The United Nations

Friend or Foe of Self-Determination?

EDITED BY

JAKOB R. AVGUSTIN

**E-INTERNATIONAL
RELATIONS
PUBLISHING**

E-International Relations
www.E-IR.info
Bristol, England
2020

ISBN 978-1-910814-48-2

This book is published under a Creative Commons CC BY-NC 4.0 license. You are free to:

- **Share** – copy and redistribute the material in any medium or format.
- **Adapt** – remix, transform, and build upon the material.

Under the following terms:

- **Attribution** – You must give appropriate credit, provide a link to the license and indicate if changes were made. You may do so in any reasonable manner, but not in any way that suggests the licensor endorses you or your use.
- **Non-Commercial** – You may not use the material for commercial purposes.

Any of the above conditions can be waived if you get permission. Please contact info@e-ir.info for any such enquiries, including for licensing and translation requests.

Other than the terms noted above, there are no restrictions placed on the use and dissemination of this book for student learning materials/scholarly use.

Production: Michael Tang
Cover Image: RonTech3000 via Shutterstock

A catalogue record for this book is available from the British Library.

E-IR Edited Collections

Series Editors: Stephen McGlinchey, Marianna Karakoulaki & Agnieszka Pikulicka-Wilczewska
Books Editor: Cameran Clayton
Editorial assistance: Benjamin Cherry-Smith and Anjasi Shah

E-IR's Edited Collections are open access scholarly books presented in a format that preferences brevity and accessibility while retaining academic conventions. Each book is available in print and digital versions, and is published under a Creative Commons license. As E-International Relations is committed to open access in the fullest sense, free electronic versions of all of our books, including this one, are available on our website.

Find out more at: http://www.e-ir.info/publications

About the E-International Relations website

E-International Relations (www.E-IR.info) is the world's leading open access website for students and scholars of international politics, reaching over 3 million unique readers annually. E-IR's daily publications feature expert articles, reviews and interviews – as well as student learning resources. The website is run by a registered non-profit organisation based in Bristol, UK and staffed with an all-volunteer team of students and scholars.

Abstract

The purpose of this edited collection is to appraise the role of the UN in relation to the principle of self-determination. This book takes a practical approach to discussing what role the UN plays in cases of self-determination and, importantly, it also ventures beyond this area's usual discussions of the inherent conflict between self-determination and sovereignty.

The chapters address the pursuit of the right to self-determination through a variety of case studies, such as post-statehood in South Sudan and East Timor; Indigenous peoples; hybrid self-determination in post-intrastate conflict; the balancing of the human rights approach in Cyprus; remedial right to secede in the cases of failed states; Palestinian and Sahrawi resistance; geopolitics in Jammu and Kashmir; and the forgotten story of micro-states. Overall, this collection shows that the solutions might be in moving the paradigm beyond the state-centrism of the system and the UN itself.

Acknowledgments

This edited collection would not exist without the support and guidance from Stephen McGlinchey, Editor-in-Chief at E-International Relations. I would also like to thank the copy-editing team, and everybody involved in editorial assistance. Mostly, I would like to thank all the contributing authors for all their hard work and patience.

Jakob R. Avgustin received his Ph.D. in International Relations from the University of Ljubljana in 2016. He is Editor-at-Large at E-International Relations and works in the Academic Services Office at the University of East Anglia. He researches the use of military force in international relations, particularly when authorised by the UN Security Council. His publications include Realism in Practice: An Appraisal (co-editor), and articles in *Sociology of Diplomacy: Initial Reading* and *Acta Diplomatica*. He is currently working on a chapter in an edited collection on Great Powers and post-Yugoslav states.

Contributors

Ed Brown is a tutor and distance learning tutor at the University of Leicester. His Ph.D. focused on secession from failed states and the ethical and pragmatic issues surrounding it. He has presented papers on self-determination, secession and state failure at several conferences, including for the British International History Group and the International Association for Peace and Conflict Studies. He has also written book reviews for journals such as the *Commonwealth Journal of International Affairs*.

Cristiana Carletti is Associate Professor of International Public Law at the Department of Political Science of Roma Tre University. She has been member of several governmental delegations taking part in international conferences and events within the United Nations, Council of Europe, European Union, and Organisation for Economic Co-operation and Development systems. She recently co-authored an article on the Global Compact on migration along the international and European perspective published in *Freedom, Security & Justice: European Legal Studies*.

Moara Assis Crivelente is a Ph.D. candidate in International Politics and Conflict Resolution at the Faculty of Economics of the University of Coimbra, Portugal. Her previous publications include a book chapter on categories of analysis of the Israeli occupation of Palestine (in Portuguese), an article on Palestinian and Saharawi participation in the UN and international solidarity as forms of resistance, and a book chapter on transitional justice in the Rwandan case.

Sheryl Lightfoot (Anishinaabe, Lake Superior Band of Ojibwe) is Canada Research Chair of Global Indigenous Rights and Politics at The University of British Columbia, where she holds academic appointments in both Political Science, the School of Public Policy and Global Affairs, and Indigenous Studies. She is also currently serving as Senior Advisor to the President on Indigenous Affairs at The University of British Columbia. Her most recent book is Global Indigenous Politics: A Subtle Revolution (Routledge Press, 2016).

David B. MacDonald is a mixed-race political science professor from Treaty 4 lands in Regina, Saskatchewan, with Trinidad Indian and Scottish ancestry. He is a full professor at the University of Guelph. His most recent books are The Sleeping Giant Awakens: Genocide, Indian Residential Schools, and the Challenge of Conciliation (University of Toronto Press, 2019), and Populism and World Politics: Exploring Inter- and Transnational Dimensions, co-edited with F.A. Stengel and D. Nabers (Palgrave MacMillan, 2019).

Tobias Nowak holds a Ph.D. in law from the University of Groningen. He works as Assistant Professor of Political Science at the Department of Transboundary Legal Studies of the Faculty of Law and at the University College of the University of Groningen. He is interested in the interaction between politics and international law. He mainly does socio-legal research on political decision-making in the European Union and on the application of EU law in the courts of the Member States.

Archie W. Simpson has been a teaching fellow in politics and international relations at a number of British universities. This includes teaching at the universities of St Andrews, Aberdeen, Stirling, Nottingham, and most recently at the University of Bath. He is also a founding member of the Centre for Small State Studies at the University of Iceland as well as a member of the international editorial board of the journal *Small States and Territories*.

Kerstin Tomiak is Assistant Professor at the Center for Peace and Human Security at the American University of Kurdistan and a postdoctoral research fellow at the Leonard Davis Institute at the Hebrew University of Jerusalem. She has worked extensively as a consultant for the North Atlantic Treaty Organisation (NATO) in Afghanistan as well as for several organisations in South Sudan. She has published in *Third World Quarterly* and is currently working on a monograph about media development in South Sudan.

Charis van den Berg is a Ph.D. candidate in law and economics at the Faculty of Law of the University of Groningen, the Netherlands. She was admitted to the selective LL.M. in legal research at the University of Groningen, specialising in international and European law. For several years she has been a researcher at the Department of Legal Theory, focusing on the right to self-determination and on aspects of self-regulation in the EU.

Stephen P. Westcott is a Postdoctoral Research Fellow at Murdoch University. His research focuses on interstate border disputes and South Asian security issues. Some of his previous articles have been published in *India Quarterly*, *Contemporary South Asia* and *The Diplomat*.

Contents

INTRODUCTION
Jakob R. Avgustin — 1

1. SELF-DETERMINATION AS A PROCESS: THE UNITED NATIONS IN SOUTH SUDAN
Kerstin Tomiak — 7

2. THE UNITED NATIONS AND SELF-DETERMINATION IN THE CASE OF EAST TIMOR
Jakob R. Avgustin — 20

3. THE UNITED NATIONS AS BOTH FOE AND FRIEND TO INDIGENOUS PEOPLES AND SELF-DETERMINATION
Sheryl Lightfoot and David B. MacDonald — 32

4. SUSTAINING PEACE AND INTERNAL SELF-DETERMINATION IN THE UN PERSPECTIVE
Cristiana Carletti — 47

5. ALTERNATIVE APPROACHES TO SELF-DETERMINATION APPLIED TO THE CYPRUS CONFLICT
Charis van den Berg and Tobias Nowak — 70

6. THE UNITED NATIONS, SELF-DETERMINATION, STATE FAILURE AND SECESSION
Ed Brown — 86

7. SELF-DETERMINATION AS RESISTANCE: SAHRAWI AND PALESTINIAN STRUGGLE FOR THE UN
Moara Assis Crivelente — 109

8. SELF-DETERMINATION AND STATE SOVEREIGNTY: THE CASE OF UN INVOLVEMENT IN JAMMU AND KASHMIR
Stephen P. Westcott — 127

9. REVISITING THE UNITED NATIONS AND THE MICRO-STATE PROBLEM
Archie W. Simpson — 144

NOTE ON INDEXING — 157

Introduction

The Precarious History of the UN towards Self-Determination

JAKOB R. AVGUSTIN

The principle of self-determination found its way into international law with Articles 1 and 55 of the United Nations (UN) Charter in 1945, followed by the UN General Assembly Declaration on the Granting of Independence to Colonial Countries and Peoples in 1960. With the Declaration on Principles of International Law concerning Friendly Relations in 1970, the UN General Assembly then expanded the concept of self-determination beyond decolonisation. However, the practical complications with sometimes violent effects of various interpretations of the concept have only been exacerbated by the 'absence of any institutional framework or guidelines for the examination of self-determination claims under international law' (Quane 1998). Despite this legal void, the UN has continued to attempt to facilitate self-determination processes in many cases. While there is some evidence that UN Security Council involvement can significantly reduce the possibility of self-determination movements 'turning violent' (Beardsley, Cunningham and White 2015), there is no comprehensive evidence characterising the general role of UN actions in upholding the principle of self-determination. The record varies for example from promises to facilitate a self-determination vote in Western Sahara to final success after massive failures in East Timor. The question therefore remains, whether the UN and its actions have enabled self-determination movements to succeed and to what degree, or whether the UN has in fact generally hindered self-determination claims contrary to its own Charter.

The purpose of this collection is therefore to appraise the role of the UN in relation to the principle of self-determination by illustrating through case studies and real-world examples. This book takes a very practical approach to discussing what role the UN has played in cases of self-determination and importantly, it also ventures beyond the usual discussions of the inherent conflict between self-determination and sovereignty. The contributing authors have looked at the application of the principle of self-determination, each through their own lens of circumstance – not just in terms of case studies presented, but in the framework used. Each chapter can be seen as a stand-alone study of the role of the UN. Though together they demonstrate a holistic representation of the complexity that is the UN and the principle of self-determination itself.

In the first chapter, Tomiak introduces self-determination as a process, arguing that the achievement of independence and sovereignty as a result of the (successful) implementation of self-determination is not and should not be understood as an endpoint. Using the example of South Sudan, Tomiak shows how internal self-determination is a continuing struggle not just in terms of all the peoples of South Sudan and the accompanying violence and power struggles, but also due to the lingering role of the UN in this post-independence phase. Similarly, R. Avgustin, in the second chapter showcasing the example of East Timor, argues that even after the independence referendum was finally held and its results implemented, the people of East Timor gained a new master in the form of the UN. In both cases, it could be concluded that the UN eventually could be understood as a friend to the principle of self-determination in terms of the two nations achieving statehood, and both cases are hailed as eventual success stories in that respect. However, both authors also uncover that the role of the UN must be appraised not only in the phases leading up to independence, but very critically also in the phases post-independence with regard to internal self-determination, i.e. sovereignty even from the UN itself.

Internal self-determination is very much at the heart of the third chapter, where Lightfoot and MacDonald look into the role of the UN when it comes to Indigenous peoples and their self-determination. Addressing how Indigenous peoples were first excluded from creating and building the UN system and then denied self-determination when the world was de-colonising, their study demonstrates how the Indigenous peoples gained influence internationally. Lightfoot and MacDonald conclude that while the UN has the potential to advance the self-determination of Indigenous peoples, its state-centrism continues to hinder that progress – for the Indigenous peoples and the UN itself. The chapter concludes with venturing even further, exploring possibilities and opportunities of future self-determination, which may involve multiple and plural sovereignties, thereby challenging the notion of state-related self-determination altogether.

In the fourth chapter, Carletti provides an in-depth exploration of the UN vision in terms of coping with post-intrastate conflict situations and the relevance of the internal pattern of self-determination, taking into account the so-called hybrid self-determination. This new interpretation of the principle has emerged as an answer to some of the past failures of sustaining peace. The last part of this chapter investigates the feasibility of this new concept and its impact on the examples of Papua New Guinea, Sri Lanka and Nepal. The impact of peace agreements which have included this hybrid self-determination component is evaluated showing the different scopes and roles the UN has/would have to adopt accordingly. These in turn set out challenges for the UN in testing and renewing its role and mandate in contemporary conflict, especially when involving a case of self-determination.

Repeatedly, it would seem that the models of external and internal self-determination might not be sufficient altogether when it comes to offering possible solutions to conflict. As argued by van den Berg and Nowak in the fifth chapter, the existing UN state-focused paradigm has been unsuccessful in bringing forward a lasting solution for the Cyprus conflict. Suggesting a shift from the current UN model, van den Berg and Nowak look beyond existing interpretations and explore the balancing approach and the human rights approach and test them on the case of Cyprus. Solving conflicts by suggesting a (UN) paradigm shift is the framework also used by Brown in the sixth chapter examining the cases of South Sudan and Somaliland. Investigating the UN stance in cases of state failure and secession, he argues that the remedial right to secede which would complement Responsibility to Protect activities could effectively be used not only to stop violence occurring due to state failure and consequent secession, but would enable the international community and the UN to approach and process cases of self-determination on a more fair basis for all parties involved. Interestingly, it seems that the 'friendliness' of the UN with regard to self-determination in cases of state failure and secession seems to wane when there is no immediate threat of violence.

This conditionality of the approach to self-determination is also explored by Crivelente in the seventh chapter. Discussions on what makes a people and how that influences the right to exercise the right to self-determination shows that the UN has been either unable or unwilling to keep decades of its own promises in the examined cases of Palestine and Western Sahara. The right to self-determination has become part of the resistance struggle and vice-versa, and the UN has been challenged not only to deal with calls for self-determination, but also with calls to respond to what is in effect ongoing colonisation. However, the UN is often locked by geopolitical considerations as is obvious also from Westcott's analysis of Jammu and Kashmir in the eighth chapter. The case study shows that while the UN advocates the right to self-determination, in practice – and especially when it comes to major states, it definitely favours the principle of territorial sovereignty. The people of

Jammu and Kashmir and their say in the matter have been ignored altogether, making the UN a foe not only regarding the right to self-determination, but also towards the violence and human rights abuses it so often condemns and deplores in its statements.

Questioning what makes a state enough of a state for the UN, opens up the discussions on the accession of micro-states to the UN as explored by Simpson in the final chapter. Sovereign and independent after de-colonisation, micro-states sought UN membership to solidify their self-determination. Despite all the discussions on size and accession criteria, as well as what constitutes full self-governance, Simpson demonstrates that in fact none of these bore an impact to their achieving UN membership. Although the process may not have been the same for accession during the Cold War and since, and even though concerns may have been genuine, in this case the UN has been successfully empowering and most clearly a friend of self-determination.

While the collection could have been a dry list of case studies, all appraising the role of the UN in the process of the right to self-determination being pursued and/or achieved, these chapters offer much more. There are critical insights into what happens after statehood is achieved, for example in South Sudan and East Timor and whether the UN continues to uphold its chartered principles. There are argumentations that the classical interpretation of self-determination, pre-determined by the system's and the UN's state-centrism which worked for the era of de-colonisation, needs to evolve to encompass the issues of today, e.g. intra-state conflict, transnational self-determination, secession from failed states, peoples and struggles that do not fit into the existing definitions. Strangely enough, it would seem that only in the case of micro-states has the UN played an active and positive role throughout. As demonstrated with examples from Papua New Guinea, Nepal and Sri Lanka, Indigenous peoples, South Sudan and Somaliland, Palestine and Western Sahara, the principle has indeed been evolving, even if with very little help and impetus from the UN itself.

Moving away from or beyond the existing UN paradigm might bring forward better and sustainable solutions for some of the longest-lasting conflicts, like the situation in Cyprus. A paradigm shift would certainly be needed for any serious renewed approaches for a UN-brokered solution in Jammu and Kashmir. As this collection is going to print, India has been actively destabilising the fragile peace currently in place by further deteriorating the status of the people in Jammu and Kashmir in spite of all its obligations under the UN Charter and numerous declarations and resolutions. This collection could have easily concluded that the role of the UN is always circumstantial, and it could have subscribed to the realist interpretation of the UN as merely a sum of its members, where the principle of territorial sovereignty and the interests of the major powers always dictate the situation. Or that self-determination only really happens when there are no perceived threats to that kind of state of affairs. Perhaps the classical 'original-sin' debate on how and why the right to self-determination inherently erodes state sovereignty should be re-defined; understanding that self-determination of the future is not necessarily state-based, as suggested, would require a very different international community and a very different UN. The most important contribution of this collection therefore lies in finding evidence of this evolving principle of self-determination and opportunities for its application beyond the existing UN paradigm.

References

Beardsley, Kevin, David E. Cunningham, and Peter B. White. 2015. "Resolving Civil Wars before They Start: The UN Security Council and Conflict Prevention in Self-Determination Disputes." *British Journal of Political Science* 47(3): 675–697.

Quane, Helen. 1998. "The United Nations and the Evolving Right to Self-Determination." *The International and Comparative Law Quarterly* 47(3): 537–572.

1

Self-Determination as a Process: The United Nations in South Sudan

KERSTIN TOMIAK

What is the United Nations' (UN) general stance on the principle of self-determination? This is a rather complicated question for several reasons. The principle itself is, as Summers (2013, 230) says, 'frustratingly ambiguous'. There can be many reasons why self-determination claims are either supported or rebuked without this hinting at a general stance of the UN, which is not a homogeneous organisation but a conglomerate of different actors and interests. Further, an examination of whether and under what conditions the organisation supported the claims alone would tell us little; just as important as the question of *if* the UN supported a self-determination claim would be the question of what happens *after* a peoples' decision, hence if the organisation values and supports a new state's independence and sovereignty. In this chapter, I argue that self-determination is not an endpoint that is reached once a people have been able to decide whether they want independence. Instead, I see self-determination as a process, which comes with the need to build a new state and state institutions. In this process of state-building, the UN quite often plays an important role. Understood in this way, insights into the organisation's stance towards self-determination that go beyond the question of whether the UN supported the original claim are achieved, as are insights about the importance of the organisation's composition. My argument is that while the UN might initially be supportive of a self-determination claim, events in a newly created state might force it to engage in behaviour that violates this state's sovereignty and shows the organisation as being unsupportive of self-determination.

In brief, I argue that (1) self-determination is a process that does not end with a declaration of independence and recognition of a new state, and (2) the stance of the UN in a self-determination case is context-dependent, with 'context' explicitly including the events in the newly created country but also the composition of the UN itself and the expectations and ideas of its individual staff. I base my argument on the case of South Sudan, where the UN was initially supportive of self-determination; nevertheless, the organisation's actions in the country following the declaration of independence showed a disregard of the new state's sovereignty. One might argue that the UN's actions were justified by the events in South Sudan with the new outbreak of violence and human suffering that came with it.

Whether or not the prevention or easing of human suffering justifies the violation of sovereignty is an important question; while a serious engagement with it is outside the scope of this chapter, it shows the dilemma the UN might be experiencing when it comes to self-determination processes. It also gives rise to possible arguments for shared sovereignty or trusteeship (Krasner 2004, 85). I am well aware that this is a slippery slope, especially in connection with self-determination claims.

Self-determination is closely linked to decolonisation (Barnsley and Bleiker 2008, 121; Del Mar 2013, 85), and a call for shared sovereignty can easily be understood as an attempt to keep a population under the thumb of either a foreign power or internal forces, and thus as re-colonisation. Further, there is a vast literature about the problems that arise when external actors engage in state-building (Bliesemann de Guevara 2008 and 2012; Bliesemann de Guevara and Kuehn 2013; Duffield 2001; Paris 2002). Nevertheless, South Sudan is but one example of self-determination that was followed by violent conflict; consequently, this has led to long-term engagements of foreign powers, which have subsequently hindered self-determination, as past elites have been exchanged for new ones. Shared sovereignty, new forms of trusteeship, predetermined timelines, previously agreed upon rights and duties of all parties involved, and a gradual transfer of power might be able to pave less rocky roads to self-determination. At least, clear terms and conditions seem more honest than the international community *de facto* running a newly independent state.

I will first give background on the principle of self-determination and South Sudan; I then turn to an examination of some of the UN's actions in the young state. I conclude by saying that while the UN supported the self-determination claim of the Southerners, it nevertheless violated the sovereignty of the young state following independence. My conclusions are based on observations and interviews during ten months of fieldwork in South Sudan in 2014 and 2015.

On the Principle of Self-Determination

Since the principle of self-determination is enshrined in the UN's Charter it would be reasonable to assume that the organisation is an advocate of the principle. Still, it does not engage in all such claims. In the past, self-determination has been linked to decolonisation and freedom from forceful, illegal occupation; this has limited the number of possible cases. The UN sometimes chooses not to engage as some cases are explicitly political, e.g. Tibet. Sometimes the organisation is blocked from engagement like in southern Yemen (Chang 1972, 37–38). Further, a conflict's history, the possibility of regional contagion and the characteristics of the dispute all play a role in the decision of whether to engage (White et al. 2018, 380). In general then, the UN, while not exactly a foe of self-determination, cannot be named a champion of the principle.

One reason for the rather wavering position is probably the composition of the organisation. Freeman (1999, 357) names it 'an association of elite states, whose primary purposes are to protect and promote the interests of their states and to maintain the existing state order. Commitments to the self-determination of *peoples* (...) are subordinate to these purposes' [italics in original]. The UN is not a homogeneous organisation; Weiss et al. (2018) distinguishes between a first, second, and third UN, thus adding to Claude's older distinction of two UNs (Claude Jr. 1996). The first UN is described as 'an institutional framework of member states' (Weiss et al. 2018, 2). The second is stated to be 'the system of decision- and policy-making by UN officials who are independent and not completely instructed by states' (Weiss et al. 2018, 4). Finally, the third is named a 'network of NGOs [non-governmental organisations], experts, corporate executives, media representatives, and academics who work closely with the first and second UN' (Weiss et al. 2018, 5). There are many actors and interests to consider before the UN can decide whether it will engage in a self-determination claim.

Further issues arise as the principle itself displays a certain degree of vagueness. It is not defined who possesses the right to self-determination (Freeman 1999, 356), and as the consequence of such a claim is often secession, the right to self-determination in principle threatens an existing state's territorial integrity (Barnsley and Bleiker 2008,125–8). Further, the threat is not only to the territorial integrity of a minority group's mother state, but to the community of states in general (Berndtsson and Johansson 2015); states' opinions on self-determination consequently differ (ibid.). Many states are home to minority groups that might want to ascend to independence and states rather avoid such claims (Koivura 2008). Therefore, consideration of a self-determination claim is not only based on the rights of the peoples but as much on the right of the state in question and the destabilisation effect the claim might have. Consequently, the right to self-determination has been named 'a variable right, [that is] depending on a combination of factors. The two most important of these seem to be the degree of destabilisation in any given claim (...), and the degree to which the responding government represents the people belonging to the territory' (Kirgis Jr. 1994, 310).

Further, ethnic groups and Indigenous peoples are rather excluded from being heard at the UN; to make their voices heard they need to borrow an identity. 'A native American would thus sit and speak as a delegate of the International Committee of Jurists or other NGO, and a Maori would relay his people's concerns in his role as a New Zealand trade unionist' (Clech Lam 1992, 617). It is the exception rather than a rule for a UN forum to permit 'concerned parties to speak in their true representative capacity' (ibid.). Henceforth, claiming the right to self-determination at the UN is rather problematic for ethnic or minority groups.

An Independent South Sudan

In the case of South Sudan these problems were overcome. The United States massively supported the Southerners' claim, based on the hope that a referendum and possible secession of the South would end the long and bloodthirsty war the country had suffered for decades. Public support, enhanced by the American film star George Clooney, also helped. In January 2011, the South held a referendum under the conditions of the 2005 *Comprehensive Peace Agreement* (CPA) and overwhelmingly decided to secede; in July 2011 independence was declared. South Sudan joined the UN shortly thereafter and became the 193rd member state of the international community of states.

Violent conflict broke out in South Sudan in December 2013 and the UN Mission in South Sudan (UNMISS) was caught off guard by this (Nzabanita 2014). UNMISS was a small mission and the lack of numbers and resources shows that the potential for conflict in the new state was – surprisingly and incorrectly – underestimated. The South is home to roughly 60 different ethnic groups. The Southern movement that drove forward the self-determination claim, the Sudan People's Liberation Army / Sudan People Liberation Movement (SPLA/SPLM), was led by Salva Kiir Mayardit (a Dinka) and Dr. Riek Machar (a Nuer), who have a well-known history of strife and quarrels (Akol 2003; Arop 2006; Johnson 2011). Following a relatively brief period of celebration, the conflict restarted, and despite a number of mediation attempts and sanctions, it is still ongoing. As this situation continued to unfold, UNMISS and other international agencies engaged and intervened in decisions concerning the sovereign Government of South Sudan (GoSS). UNMISS was originally mandated to support the GoSS in areas such as good governance, security-sector reform and establishing the rule of law (S/RES/1996). Following the outbreak of violent conflict, the mandate changed to focus on the protection of civilians (S/RES/2406).

The UN, the International Community, and the Dilemma of Self-Determination

It is not unusual for the UN to stay on after a self-determination claim and referendum. In Timor-Leste, which voted for secession from Indonesia in 1999 and became independent in 2002, the UN took over administration as the new state needed to be built from scratch following an outbreak of massive violence by pro-Indonesian militia and the Indonesian army (S/RES/1272). The mandate the UN Security Council gave to the UN Transitional Administration in East Timor (UNTAET) was broad, however, and 'left several key questions unanswered, including the roadmap leading to self-government, the relationship of the governance and public administration component to the future East Timorese government, and the mechanism for consultation with the East Timorese' (Martin and Mayer-Riek 2005, 133). Chesterman (2002, 63–4) argues that 'many of the expatriates working for UNTAET and the 70-odd international NGOs tend to treat the Timorese political system as a *tabula rasa*', an approach that effectively excluded the Timorese from their state-building project.

In South Sudan, where the UN's mandate was nowhere near as broad, a similar tendency could be observed. Autesserre (2014) has described that international expatriates, working for international organisations and NGOs, value technical expertise over local knowledge and reproduce the systems they are most familiar with. This might be a reason for the tendency of UN personnel to ask counterparts in host governments for certain behaviours – a tendency that is understood as dictating behaviours and policies in these host governments. Furthermore, the relationship between the international community and a host government is asymmetrical, with one party providing, the other receiving funds. In South Sudan, this led to conflicting ideas of each party what the other was entitled to, which led to the deterioration of the relationship between the parties, as I will show in the next section.

The UN's Behaviour in South Sudan

The problems between the GoSS and the UN were probably most apparent in what can be named the 'Toby Lanzer incident'. In May 2015, the GoSS expelled the UN's resident relief coordinator Toby Lanzer. This was due to

Lanzer's media activities; in particular, an interview given in Geneva, Switzerland in which Lanzer had critiqued the South Sudanese government harshly and described it as a failure. Supporting reasons were his critical tweets and statements on social media where Lanzer is said to have stated that South Sudan was on the brink of bankruptcy (Atem 2015). Ateny Wek Ateny, spokesperson of the GoSS, said in an interview with the newspaper *The Citizen*, 'These statements are irresponsible statements from the humanitarian coordinator, given the fact that they don't give hope to the people of South Sudan' (ibid.). Expelling Toby Lanzer generated turmoil in the international community. International actors saw their opinion of the South Sudanese government as ruthless and authoritarian confirmed. Then UN Secretary-General Ban Ki-moon condemned the decision, named Lanzer 'instrumental in addressing the increasing humanitarian needs of conflict-affected communities in the country' (United Nations 2015), called on the GoSS to reverse the decision immediately, and urged the government to 'cooperate fully with all United Nations entities present in South Sudan' (ibid.).

The South Sudanese government felt unfairly criticised by Lanzer and reacted by expelling him. This was certainly not a wise decision and probably an overreaction; nevertheless, the GoSS was within its rights to do so. The UN Secretary-General, however, requested the government of an independent sovereign country to revoke its decision and to cooperate with the UN, which was read by the government and by many South Sudanese as a call to obey the UN. This did not bode well with the government. The GoSS views the UN and the international donors and expat community as guests in the country; as such 'they do have to obey the rules of South Sudan and not make their own rules. They have to follow our rules'.[1] The international community on the other hand, viewed itself as supporting the country and as having a voice in how it is run. A civil servant from the European Union stated in an informal discussion that 'governments come and go. We assist the people of South Sudan'.[2] The same was, phrased in different ways, stated by employees of international nongovernmental organisations (iNGOs) in the country. The international community feels that because of the amount of money they are giving they have a say in the country's governance. Most prominently, this was phrased by an acquaintance working for an iNGO, who said: 'We have literally paid for everything in this country. This country is functioning only because of us'.[3]

The GoSS on the other hand, does not see a connection between receiving

---

[1] Interview with a South Sudanese government official in the Ministry of Information and Broadcast, conducted in Juba, 30 June 2015.
[2] Field notes, 16 April 2015.
[3] Field notes, 23 February 2015.

donor money and a right to decide. In informal talks, government officials said that they are happy to receive advice, but they do not feel an obligation to take it. In this regard, it was also quite often stated that foreign experts and UN workers, as well as iNGO employees, are rather clueless about realities in the country. An explanation for this might be the way the donors and expat workers live and work. What has been described as 'the expat bubble' makes for a tangible barrier between foreigners and the South Sudanese and has an effect on the perceptions of the other group (Autesserre 2014; Smirl 2015). There is a clear tendency of 'bunkerisation' (Fisher 2017), with foreigners living and working for security reasons in secure compounds with very limited connections to the outside world. The high levels of security for the compounds of foreigners, including the UN agencies, make for divisions; government officials repeatedly phrased a general feeling of mistrust when talking about their relationship with foreigners.

While this points to a more general problem in the relationship between the international community and a host government, a clearer violation of the GoSS's sovereignty was the interference of UNMISS in the government's media policy. In February 2015, the Minister for Information, Michael Makuei, threatened to close the UN's Radio Miraya. Miraya had aired an interview with an exiled politician, namely Rebecca Garang, who was placed under house arrest in December 2013, before she went into exile. Makuei named her a rebel and threatened to shut down the UN's radio station. The threat was retracted after the intervention of Ellen Margrethe Løj, the then head of UNMISS. Like the Toby Lanzer incident, the Miraya incident was interpreted in two different ways. While almost every international worker in South Sudan who I talked to understood it as an affront of the government against press freedom and the UN in general, South Sudanese acquaintances were taken aback by what they described as 'another UNMISS-arrogance'.[4] It was said that no government in the West would allow a radio station to air rebel views and that the UN needed to follow the laws in the country.[5]

The two occurrences had a similar pattern. A member or an institution of the international community states or broadcasts something the government of the host country understands as hostile; it reacts to this and is rebuffed by the international actor and made to reverse its decision. The concern here is not if the reaction of the GoSS in both cases was appropriate – this is certainly debatable. The concern is that the decision of a sovereign government was overrun by an actor that is supposed to support the self-determination of people. Instead, both incidents show the UN pushing for the GoSS to behave

---

[4] Interview with a South Sudanese media consultant and advisor, conducted in Juba, 20 June 2015.

[5] Ibid.

as they, the UN, saw fit.

This struggle over predominance between the local elites and the international actors was further apparent in the international community's reaction to the GoSS's attempt to regulate iNGOs. In May 2015, the government issued a new bill that required them to register with the government: a tedious and costly process but not a new or unusual requirement. Furthermore, it ordered iNGOs to ensure that no more than a fifth of their staff were foreigners. This caused concern among the iNGOs working in South Sudan. It was claimed that this regulation would result in delays of projects because of a shortage of skilled South Sudanese workers. This was dismissed by nationals. 'We do not have a capacity problem', I was told, '...we have a capacity utilisation problem'.[6] Another statement was that 'the international community is doing capacity building here since ten years. How can there not be enough capacity? Did they do something wrong?'[7] The government and many well-educated South Sudanese have long been complaining that iNGOs give too many jobs to foreigners instead of to the local population. The NGO bill with its quota for foreigners was seen as reasonable and necessary by them and the argument of the internationals that there are not enough skilled people for employment in South Sudan was understood as an insult. In the end however, the GoSS partly retracted the bill in explaining that it concerned only certain professions and management levels and the quotas were not enforced.

The meddling of foreigners in internal affairs was also apparent when six US-based iNGOs, including Human Rights Watch, sent a letter to John Kerry, the then US Secretary of State, and asked for more sanctions against South Sudan to force the warring parties to strike a peace deal. Surely this was well meant, but it did not soften the GoSS's approach towards iNGOs or foreigners. According to the *New Nation*, a South Sudanese newspaper, it was seen as a 'blatant interference in the internal affairs of a sovereige nation'.[8] The government reacted by saying that the iNGOs should rather 'reflect on their current soft-gloves approach towards the rebels and start to exercise more pressure on the rebels to motivate them to return to the peace talks'.[9] This, to be sure, was not the UN or one of its agencies behaving in this way, but using the notion of the 'third UN', the network of iNGOs working with the UN (Weiss et al. 2018), the problem of the international community meddling in the internal affairs of a sovereign country is evident.

---

[6] Interview with a South Sudanese project manager, conducted in Juba, 18 April 2015.
[7] Interview with a South Sudanese advisor, conducted in Juba, 12 August 2015.
[8] New Nation newspaper, 17 June 2015.
[9] Ibid.

Friend or Foe?

Where does all this leave us with the question of whether the UN is a friend or foe of self-determination? This question can be answered from two different angles. One can examine if and for what reasons the organisation gets involved in self-determination claims. This perspective sees self-determination as a result. Self-determination can, however, also be seen as a process. In this view, it is not achieved by just a popular vote and a (possible) declaration of independence. Instead, self-determination would be achieved when there is a functioning state in place, a state that is grounded in its peoples' decisions and whose acts are respected by the international community. Such a state cannot be declared, instead, it needs to be built. How the UN engages in this process provides a different answer to the question of whether it is a friend or a foe of self-determination. Thinking about self-determination as a result, South Sudan would count as a rather successful case; independence was declared following a popular vote. If seen as a process, South Sudan is not a successful case as its declaration of independence was followed by a power struggle, outbreak of violent conflict, and human suffering; it can certainly not be declared that the peoples of South Sudan have achieved self-determination. Questions about the UN's stance towards South Sudan's sovereignty also arise. The UN, mandated at first with supporting the GoSS and later with the protection of civilians, butted heads with the government about how certain aspects of governance should be managed, giving room to the accusation that the organisation might be supportive only of a certain kind of state. In Timor-Leste, the organisation that enjoyed a much broader mandate was also accused of not engaging and consulting enough with the local people but running the country as it saw fit (Chesterman 2002, 64–68).

Sticking to the notion of the first, the second, and the third UN is helpful here. As introduced by Weiss et al. (2018, 2), these include the member states, the system of UN-officials and the network of NGOs, consultants and journalists working for the UN. In the case of South Sudan, the first UN was positively engaged in the self-determination of the South. After the declaration of independence and the recognition of South Sudan as a sovereign state, the second and the third UN engaged in practices that can be understood as a violation of sovereignty. This was due to events in the country. With this, it can be said that parts of the UN were a friend while others were a foe. The stance of the UN towards self-determination is not necessarily homogenous.

Stephen Krasner (2004, 85) states that the rules of what he calls 'conventional sovereignty', including the principle of non-interference in the internal affairs of a sovereign state, are frequently violated in practice. In the case of South Sudan, the interference of the international community can be seen as justified by the dire situation in the country. Personally, I do not doubt that the UN-personnel in South Sudan genuinely acted with the best interests of the South Sudanese people at heart. Still, it seems unclear how interference in the media and in the government's decision to regulate iNGOs working in the country would be able to end the conflict or ease human suffering. Instead, these interferences worsened the relationship between the government and the international community and contributed to growing mistrust between the parties. With these practices, the UN acted more like a foe to the process of self-determination.

It is not a rare occurrence that self-determination is followed by violent conflict and this begs the question of if there is a way to cope with self-determination to solve or prevent such situations. Shared sovereignty or trusteeships have been proposed (Krasner 2004). With reference to a people who want to decide their fate, this seems unreasonable; still, in cases of potentially weak, new states in conflict or in danger thereof, there might be a point in question. In South Sudan, self-determination was guaranteed only to have it violated by external powers. These interferences did not help overcome the conflict; instead, they caused ongoing mistrust and problems between the actors involved. Further research might clarify if agreements about shared sovereignty or a trusteeship with mutually agreed clear guidelines on such points as the partners' responsibilities, complaint mechanisms, and length of the agreement might be better policy tools to overcome or prevent violent conflict and help new states on their way to self-determination.

References

Akol, Lam. 2003. *SPLM/SPLA: The Nasir Declaration*. New York: iUniverse.com.

Arop, Madut Arop. 2015. *Sudan's Painful Road to Peace. A Full Story of the Founding and Development of SPLM/SPLA*. North Charleston, South Carolina: BookSurge LLC.

Atem, Ayuen Akuot. 2015. "UN Aid Chief Expelled as Western Countries Voice Concern." *The Citizen*, June 3, 2015.

Autesserre, Séverine. 2014. *Peaceland: Conflict Resolution and the Everyday Politics of International Intervention. Problems of International Politics*. Cambridge: Cambridge University Press.

Barnsley, Ingrid, and Roland Bleiker. 2008. "Self-Determination: From Decolonization to Deterritorialization." *Global Change, Peace & Security* 20 (2): 121–136. https://doi.org/10.1080/14781150802079797.

Berndtsson, Joakim, and Peter Johansson. 2015. "Principles on a Collision Course? State Sovereignty meets Peoples' Right of Self-Determination in the Case of Kosovo." *Cambridge Review of International Affairs* 28 (3): 445–461. https://doi.org/10.1080/09557571.2014.942724.

Bliesemann de Guevara, Berit. 2008. "The State in Times of Statebuilding." *Civil Wars* 10 (4): 348–368. https://doi.org/10.1080/13698240802354466.

Bliesemann de Guevara, Berit. 2012. "Introduction: Statebuilding and State-Formation." In *Statebuilding and State-Formation. The Political Sociology of Intervention*, edited by Berit Bliesemann de Guevara, 1–18. London: Routledge.

Bliesemann de Guevara, Berit, and Florian Kuehn. 2013. "The Political Economy of Statebuilding: Rents, taxes and Perpetual Dependency." In *Routledge Handbook of International Statebuilding*, edited by David Chandler and Timothy Sisk, 219–230. London: Routledge.

Chang, King-yuh. 1972. "The United Nations and Decolonization: The Case of Southern Yemen." *International Organization* 26 (1): 37–61.

Chesterman, S. 2002. "East Timor in Transition: Self-Determination, State-Building and the United Nations." *International Peacekeeping* 9 (1): 45–76. https://doi.org/10.1080/714002704.

Claude, Inis L. 1996. "Peace and Security: Prospective Roles for the Two United Nations." *Global Governance* 2 (3): 289–298. http://www.jstor.org/stable/27800143

Del Mar, Katherine. 2013. "The Myth of Remedial Secession." In *Statehood and Self-Determination. Reconciling Tradition and Modernity in International Law*, edited by Duncan French, 79–108. Cambridge: Cambridge University Press.

Duffield, Marc. 2001. *Global Governance and the New Wars*. London: Zed Books.

Fisher, Jonathan. 2017. "Reproducing remoteness? States, internationals and the co-constitution of aid 'bunkerization' in the East African periphery." *Journal of Intervention and Statebuilding* 11 (1): 98–119.
https://doi.org/10.1080/17502977.2016.1260209.

Freeman, Michael. 1999. "The right to self-determination in international politics: six theories in search of a policy." *Review of International Studies* 25 (3): 355–370. Johnson, Douglas H. 2011. *The Root Causes of Sudan's Civil wars: Peace or Truce*. Woodbridge, Suffolk: James Currey.

Kirgis, Frederic L. 1994. "The Degrees of Self-Determination in the United Nations Era." *The American Journal of International Law* 88 (2): 304–310.

Koivurova, Timo. 2008. "From High Hopes to Disillusionment: Indigenous Peoples' Struggle to (re)Gain Their Right to Self-determination." *International Journal on Minority and Group Rights* 15 (1): 1–26.

Krasner, Stephen D. 2004. "Sharing Sovereignty: New Institutions for Collapsed and Failing States." *International Security* 29 (2): 85–120.

Lam, Maivan Clech. 1992. "Making Room for Peoples at the United Nations: Thoughts Provoked by Indigenous Claims to Self-Determination." *Cornell International Law Journal* 25, no. 7 (3): 604–622.

Martin, Ian, and Alexander Mayer-Rieckh. 2005. "The United Nations and East Timor: from self-determination to state-building." *International Peacekeeping* 12 (1): 125–145. https://doi.org/10.1080/135333104200028659 5.

Nzabanita, Priscilla. 2014. "South Sudan Crisis brings Questions for UNMISS." *IPI Global Observatory*, March 14, 2014.
https://theglobalobservatory.org/2014/03/unmiss-south-sudan-violence/.

Paris, Roland. 2002. "International peacebuilding and the 'mission civilisatrice'." *Review of International Studies* 28 (4): 637–656.
https://doi.org/10.1017/S026021050200637X.

Smirl, Lisa. 2015. *Spaces of Aid: How Cars, Compounds and Hotels Shape Humanitarianism*. London: Zed Books.

Summers, James. 2013. "The International and External Aspects of Self-Determination Reconsidered." In *Statehood and Self-Determination. Reconciling Tradition and Modernity in International Law*, edited by Duncan French, 229–249. Cambridge: Cambridge University Press.

United Nations, Department of Public Information, *Statement attributable to the Spokesman for the Secretary-General on South Sudan*. 01 June 2015, available from https://www.un.org/sg/en/content/sg/statement/2015-06-01/statement-attributable-spokesman-secretary-general-south-sudan.

United Nations Security Council Resolution 1272 (1999), *East Timor*, S/RES/1272 (25 October 1999), available from https://undocs.org/S/RES/1272(1999).

United Nations Security Council Resolution 1996 (2011), *Reports of the Secretary-General on the Sudan*, S/RES/1996 (08 July 2011), available from https://undocs.org/S/RES/1996(2011).

United Nations Security Council Resolution 2406 (2018), *Reports of the Secretary-General on the Sudan and South Sudan*, S/RES/2406 (15 March 2018), available from https://undocs.org/S/RES/2406(2018).

Weiss, Thomas G., David P. Forsythe, Roger P. Coate, and Kelly-Kate Pease. 2018. *The United Nations and Changing World Politics*. 8th ed. London: Routledge.

White, Peter B, David E Cunningham, and Kyle Beardsley. 2018. "Where, when, and how does the UN work to prevent civil war in self-determination disputes?" *Journal of Peace Research* 55 (3): 380–394. https://doi.org/10.1177/0022343317744826.

2

The United Nations and Self-Determination in the Case of East Timor

JAKOB R. AVGUSTIN

This chapter will look at a case study of self-determination which became prominent in the UN in the 1970s and was only indirectly linked to the process of decolonisation as such. Portugal as a colonial power either neglected East Timor[1] or ruled with a heavy hand, leaving its people to eventually gain independence from decades of violence under Indonesian occupation. This chapter will not discuss the different definitions of self-determination or the historic development of this legal right. However, it will discuss the story of East Timor, highlighting the practice of the UN, particularly through the resolutions of the Security Council (SC), and assess the role of the UN from that perspective. Self-determination is understood in this chapter purely normatively – as a right of any people to declare and establish a sovereign and independent political entity. The underlying assumption being that given the UN, and the SC especially, is a political organisation, the road to the eventual outcome for East Timor is not expected to even appear straightforward. In fact, as this chapter will show, at times the UN actively obstructed the claim of the East Timorese people for their sovereignty, casting serious doubt on the organisation's supposedly favourable stance towards self-determination of peoples.

Short History

The small island of Timor, situated only about 500km north of Australia, has

---

Officially the Democratic Republic of Timor-Leste since 2002, however this chapter will use East Timor throughout.

spent most of its history at the crossroads between major powers dominating maritime southeast Asia; it was first used as a trading post for China and India, and then in the seventeenth century the western part became colonised by the Dutch while the Portuguese took over the eastern part of the island. The Portuguese were not very efficient in establishing governance which resulted in two parallel systems of rule – the colonial and the indigenous one (Taylor 1994, 12). Even though the *Sentenca Arbitral* codified the border between the eastern and the western part of the island in 1915, the Timorese people all over the island fought the occupation by Japan in World War II with guerrilla tactics under the leadership of Australian commandos (Taylor 1994, 12–13). Even though Australia left the island in 1943, the Timorese continued their guerrilla fighting on the side of the Allies until the end of the war and at a high human life cost (Taylor 1994, 13). Despite their efforts and sacrifice, the island remained divided between two foreign masters after the war – the western part was incorporated into Indonesia while the eastern part remained under rather uninterested Portuguese administration which nonetheless used violence to rule. In the 1970s, as a civil war broke out between the pro-Portuguese and pro-independence movements in their Timorese colony, the Portuguese simply left, burdened by the coup d'état in their homeland (Calvocoressi 2001, 561). Despite official assurances in April 1974 that they would not interfere with the Portuguese Timor (Taylor 1994, 25), Indonesia took advantage of the opportunity and annexed the eastern part of the island, although neither the UN nor Portugal ever recognised this annexation. It is at that point that the situation of East Timor appears in the UN SC documents for the first time.

In fact, in its very first resolution on East Timor S/RES/384 (1975) the UN SC recognises 'the inalienable right of the people of East Timor to self-determination and independence in accordance with the principles of the Charter of the United Nations and the Declaration on the Granting of Independence to Colonial Countries and Peoples, contained in the General Assembly (GA) Resolution 1514 (XV) of 14 December 1960'. The UN SC was also 'gravely concerned about the deterioration of the situation' and the loss of life in East Timor, and deplored the 'intervention of the armed forces of Indonesia in East Timor'. It even regretted that 'the government of Portugal did not discharge fully its responsibilities as administering Power in the Territory'. The UN SC at that point called 'all States to respect the territorial integrity of East Timor as well as the inalienable right of its people to self-determination', and called upon Indonesia to withdraw and upon Portugal to cooperate fully with the UN so as to enable the people of East Timor to exercise freely their right to self-determination'. It also requested the UN Secretary-General to send a to East Timor for on-spot assessment. The UN GA also adopted its first resolution on East Timor in 1975 and then adopted a further resolution each year, all of which basically echoed the UN SC resolutions, but only until 1982.

Clear and unequivocal support of the UN SC for recognising the inalienable right of the people of East Timor to self-determination and independence continued in the following year with S/RES/389 (1976) reaffirming the previous resolution. The UN SC again called upon 'all States to respect the territorial integrity of East Timor as well as the inalienable right of its people to self-determination' and called upon 'Indonesia to withdraw without further delay all its forces from the Territory'. It also requested that the Special Representative of the UN Secretary-General continue their assignment. However, it is important to note at this point that S/RES/384 was adopted unanimously while S/RES/389 was adopted with Japan and the US abstaining, signalling their alliance with the strategically positioned Indonesia.

The next time the UN SC or the UN GA addressed the issue of East Timor wasn't until 1999. In the two decades of Indonesian rule, the people of East Timor were subjected to violence and isolation with about 80% of the male population killed in the first months of the occupation (Taylor 1994, 68) and almost a quarter of the population dying of disease or hunger according to the Commission for Reception, Truth and Reconciliation in East Timor (Chega! 2008). It seems as if the international community with all its institutions simply forgot about East Timor, even though in 1979 the president and his deputy were killed (Calvocoressi 2001, 561) and the agriculture economy and infrastructure in East Timor were practically destroyed (Taylor 1994, ix). Even the International Committee of the Red Cross didn't conduct any operations in East Timor until 2002. Even more, the UN Secretary-General Special Representative was denied access to areas in question and it seems as if there was an active effort of the West to support Indonesia and Suharto's regime and keep East Timor off the agenda (Calvocoressi 2001; Wheeler and Dunne 2001) despite incredible human rights violations and violence against the Timorese people.

Suharto, President of Indonesia from 1967 to 1998, was determined to quash any resistance in East Timor and was implicitly supported by the West with the US and the UK regularly supplying the Indonesian military (Calvocoressi 2001, 561). The international community definitely played a role in keeping East Timor off the agenda in terms of maintaining international peace and security for more than 20 years. Indonesia was an important strategic ally of the West during the Cold War and half of a small island in Southeast Asia and its people were not. Australia, its closest Western neighbour, was fully aware of Indonesia's plans to invade (Wheeler and Dunne 2008, 806) and in fact accepted the legitimacy of Indonesia's rule and even used its influence to smooth out criticism of Indonesia in the UN (Wheeler and Dunne 2001, 810).

Even more, it seems Australia actively prevented the UN Secretary-General Special Representative to establish contact with the 'rebel' areas by seizing the radio transmitter with the order coming directly from the Australian Prime Minister (Taylor 1994, 72).

Nonetheless, many efforts were being undertaken in the background, particularly towards resolving the role of Portugal and its relationship with Indonesia. Even though Indonesia *de facto* administered the territory, Portugal still felt it had a right in deciding the destiny of East Timor despite the decision of the International Court of Justice in the Case Concerning East Timor (Portugal V. Australia) in 1995 which found that East Timor is a territory without self-government and the East Timorese are a people with a right to self-determination.

The Road to the Referendum

With Suharto's resignation in 1998, the ideas of independence gained new ground among the East Timorese and the new Indonesian President Habibie turned out to be a proponent of the idea of more autonomy for East Timor, even if not sovereignty. Further discussions between Indonesia and Portugal resulted in an agreement for an independence referendum to be organised under the auspices of the UN. However, it wasn't until May 1999 that Indonesia and Portugal signed the so-called *General Agreement* on the question of East Timor which then led to the report from the UN Secretary-General proposing an independence referendum and a UN observer mission which the UN SC enacted in the S/RES/1246 on 11 June 1999 with the establishment of the UN Assistance Mission in East Timor (UNAMET) which was established to assist with the organisation, implementation and supervision of the referendum on 8 August 1999. After 23 years of not having had the question of East Timor on its agenda, the UN SC suddenly became much more responsive to the developments in East Timor, adopting five further resolutions in that year.

Despite threats and intimidation, 98% of registered voters took part and 78.5% voted in favour of independence (Chesterman 2007, 194). What followed immediately however was a repetition of old behaviour from Indonesia – militias wreaked havoc in waves of violence, which might have indeed been coordinated from Indonesian governmental circles (Chesterman 2007, 195). Approximately 30,000 people were killed with thousands fleeing for their lives (Calvocoressi 2001, 562). It must be pointed out that the UN, i.e. the international observers, in fact expected and warned of unrest and conflict following the referendum, yet the UN sent only a small force of 300 military troops and 400 police officers to that end (Paris 2001, 773). With this in mind, one could argue that the UN had indeed not learned much from the tragic experience in Rwanda, nor applied any of these lessons when it came to future cases of self-determination, for example in Sudan/South Sudan.

After the Referendum

Discussing why such grave failures in organising, observing and safeguarding the independence referendum process have occurred and whose responsibility they were, is beyond the scope of this chapter. However, they must be acknowledged as despite all the paperwork adopted via the UN, i.e. reports by the UN Secretary-General, and UN SC and UN GA resolutions, tens of thousands of East Timorese died as a result of those failures before and shortly after the independence referendum in August 1999. Some claim that this inability or even incapability of UN Secretariat bureaucrats to foresee and prevent such violence constitutes gross neglect (Bolton 2001, 142). With the UN SC permanent members tired of sending their troops all over the world throughout the 1990s, it was almost miraculous and indeed unprecedented that within three weeks of the referendum being held, a peace enforcement mission led by Australia had been established by the UN SC with S/RES/1264 (1999), and had indeed already been marching into the East Timor capital of Dili. What is even more impressive about this case is that the peace enforcement operation was undertaken with agreement of the 'aggressor' – even though Indonesia's agreement would not have been necessary for such action with UN SC authorisation.

The International Force for East Timor (INTERFET) was authorised under Chapter VII of the UN Charter and was authorised to use all necessary means to fulfil its mandate 'to restore peace and security in East Timor, to protect and support UNAMET in carrying out its tasks and, within force capabilities, to facilitate humanitarian assistance operations'. To demonstrate how acute the situation in East Timor was in terms of the UN SC response, it must be explained that the case of East Timor is one in only four instances where the UN SC determined under Chapter VII of the Charter that the situation constituted a threat to international peace and security, established a multinational military peace enforcement operation (not conducted under the UN flag), and authorised the use of all necessary means – all in the first resolution addressing the outburst of violence (R. Avgustin 2016).[2] In six weeks, INTERFET took charge of all critical points with Indonesian military retreating even before INTERFET units reached all parts of the territory. It took, however, two further UN missions – UN Transitional Administration in

---

[2] The other three in the period till 2012 were *Operation Uphold Democracy* led by the US in Haiti in 1994, *Multi-National Force – Iraq* led by the US in Iraq in 2003, and *Multinational Interim Force* led by the US in Haiti in 2004 (R. Avgustin 2016, 95).

East Timor (UNTAET) and UN Mission of Support in East Timor (UNMISET) – and almost three more years for East Timor to become an independent and sovereign country on 20 May 2002. In the same month, the UN GA also adopted a resolution with which it removed East Timor from its list of non-self-governing territories (A/RES/56/282). In September 2002, East Timor became a Member State of the UN (A/RES/57/3).

UNMISET was replaced by the UN Office in Timor-Leste (UNOTIL) in 2005 which was replaced by the UN Integrated Mission in Timor-Leste (UNMIT) in 2006. Importantly, when new outbursts of violence occurred in 2006, East Timor did not make a plea for help at the UN but went directly to Australia, which again obliged with a new and, again, successful military operation. Operation *Astute* which completed its mission in 2013 included Portuguese troops who interestingly remained under their own chained command. The operation was not directly authorised by the UN SC, however it was given full support and acknowledgment *post festum* in 2006 with S/RES/1690.

From Independence to Sovereignty

In the process of declaring independence from effectively two masters, it would seem that East Timor gained a third one – the UN itself. The UN SC and all the missions it authorised practically took over the country and ran it for another decade after the independence referendum. UNTAET which was authorised to use all necessary means to fulfil its mandate was granted power and authority over the entire legislative and executive branches as well as administration over the judiciary. Since UNTAET completed its mandate in a territory where there was no effective governance, or at least none that could satisfy the UN expectations, there might be room to understand the UNTAET mandate. Yet, UNMISET which took over in 2002 had a similarly broad mandate and was also authorised to use all necessary means. UN bureaucrats even negotiated internationally on behalf of East Timor (Chesterman 2007, 19). However, one should also take into account numerous pleas of East Timor's representatives for UN missions to be prolonged and/or strengthened; for example the Foreign Minister's February 2004 request that the UN SC extend the mandate of UNMISET, or the letter from the Prime Minister in January 2005 in which he requested the continued presence of the UN. In fact, UNOTIL was established in 2005 following a proposal from the Prime Minister – it was then that this *de facto* UN administration softened into a political mission which supports further development of state institutions, democratic values, rule of law, and the promotion of human rights. This mandate continued with UNMIT until 2012 when it completed its mandate. It was in 2012 that the UN SC and the UN GA also adopted the last of their resolutions regarding East Timor. From 1999 to

2012 the UN SC adopted 25 resolutions[3] regarding East Timor, the Secretary-General wrote more than 40 reports for the UN SC, and the UN GA adopted 36 resolutions.

Evaluating the Role of the UN

Analysis of the UN and its role in the international community can often be reduced to debates on its legitimacy and legality (De Wet 2004; Blokker 2005; Manusama 2006; Thakur 2006; Hurd 2007; Cronin and Hurd 2008; Dedring 2008) which lie at the heart of the debate on whether the UN is indeed merely a sum of its members. The theoretical frameworks underpinning explanations on both sides of that debate nonetheless do not provide any practical guidelines on how to evaluate the role of the UN and its actions. In fact, it would seem that up until the moment an action is discussed, most will argue about positions of certain member states, particularly the permanent members of the UN SC. It is only at the point when an action, i.e. resolution, is adopted that opinions begin referring to the effectiveness, purpose, responsibility, and even cost-efficiency of the UN as such.

Reasons for the prevalently unfavourable opinions vary widely; increasing membership (Snow and Brown 1996; Ziring et al. 2005), more complex notions of security (Roper 1993; Rothgeb 1993; Cortright and Lopez 2002; Smillie and Minear 2004; Thakur 2006; Trent 2007; Roberts and Zaum 2008), changed international relations due to new/different actors (Rothgeb 1993; Rupesinghe and Anderlini 1998; Hirst 2001; Malone 2004; Schoenbaum 2006; Trent 2007; Richmond 2008), changes regarding the nature of armed conflict (Snow and Brown 1996; Galtung et al. 2002; Roberts and Zaum 2008), a non-functioning UN SC during the Cold War (Roper 1993; Kegley and Raymond 1994; Snow and Brown 1996; Ryan 2000; Weiss and Collins 2000; Cortright and Lopez 2002; Malone 2004; Roberts and Zaum 2008), and even unclear provisions of the UN Charter (Bailey and Daws 1998). Discussions on cases of self-determination inherently expose the internal clash of the UN Charter between the principles of sovereignty and self-determination. That in itself makes for a troubling starting point in evaluating the role of the UN in such cases as favouring one principle inevitably makes the UN deny the other, almost as if it were a zero-sum game.

Evaluating the case of East Timor through the perspective of the UN SC permanent members is interesting as this tiny island really hasn't been of strategic interest to any of them. However, Indonesia was very much a strategic ally, particularly for the West and Australia. That state of affairs was

---

[3] For comparison, the UN SC adopted altogether 23 resolutions regarding Rwanda (excluding the ones referring to the International Criminal Tribunal for Rwanda).

important enough that the UN as well as the UN SC permanent members turned a blind eye to blatant human rights violations and suffering. Then, in the late 1990s, the balance shifted – first with Suharto's departure, but more importantly, with a significant change in Australia's public opinion. Indonesia's new President Habibie was going to consider increased autonomy for East Timor, but then-Australian Prime Minister Howard suggested postponing a referendum for another decade (McDougall 2007, 872). Australia hadn't been a big proponent of self-determination as such until that point anyway (Woodard 1999, 9), but the Australian public was appalled and consequently demonstrated enough pressure to have the Australian Government offer to lead INTERFET (McDougall 2007, 873). Due to media exposure even the US ended up contributing some troops and logistical support (Strobel 2001, 684). Notably however, Australian foreign policy shifted from a clear strategic and trade interest with Indonesia to connecting humanitarian and legal norms with concepts of national interest (Woodard 1999, 10). However, one shouldn't forget that East Timor most likely remains very interesting to Australia also because of its oil reserves.

Concluding Remarks

The case of East Timor does not provide a clear and definitive answer as to whether the UN has been a friend or foe overall. The UN definitely counts East Timor as one of its most successful cases and East Timor is a peaceful and stable country today, but one should understand that the UN became successful only after the people of East Timor finally voted for their own independence and due to a member state, whose own people demanded a significant change and military action. Now, it is important that the UN SC or any of the permanent members didn't stand in the way of that action – this is where East Timor could be counted as 'lucky' to have been of no strategic interest to any of them.

That position was also extremely unfortunate for the people of East Timor in the decades of Portuguese violent neglect and Indonesian brutality. In those years, the UN definitely was not upholding the right to self-determination for East Timorese, nor was it upholding any of the several (universal) declarations, resolutions and practices which were applied in several other situations, more or less successfully. It would seem that from the standpoint of the UN SC permanent members, East Timor just never quite made it to the top of the priorities list, particularly after the end of the Cold War when so many threats to international peace and security were dealt with. For example, the military action in Kosovo was taking place at roughly the same time. The French Ambassador to the UN at the time stated that the conflict over East Timor is an "orphan of the Cold War, where the interests of the major powers are circumstantial at best" (Carey and Walsh 2008, 355). However, even in 1999 with all the lessons of Somalia, Rwanda, former Yugoslavia, and others, the UN went to East Timor practically blind and deaf to all the warning signs. Once again, even though the referendum indeed took place, the UN failed the people of East Timor. Was it because the UN was pre-occupied with more 'important' events around the world once again, or was it because the UN SC permanent members were getting tired of policing those events around the world?

It would seem that the UN cannot be a friend or a foe to self-determination as such until its members, particularly the UN SC permanent members, or a strong enough 'outsider' like Australia in the case of East Timor, make it one or the other. Importantly though in the case of East Timor, it could be argued that the UN was definitely not a friend to the people of East Timor even without the right to self-determination in the equation. It is in this conclusion that the true incapability of the UN lies and continues to be present around the world.

References

Bailey, Sydney D., and Sam Daws. 1998. *The Procedure of the UN Security Council*. 3rd edition. Oxford: Oxford University Press.

Blokker, Niels. 2005. "The Security Council and the use of force: On recent practice." In *The Security Council and the Use of Force. Theory and Reality – A Need for Change?*, edited by Niels Blokker and Nico Schrijver, 1–31. Leiden: Martinues Nijhoff Publishers.

Bolton, John R. 2001. "United States Policy on United Nations Peacekeeping: Case Studies in the Congo, Sierra Leone, Ethiopia-Eritrea, Kosovo, and East Timor." *World Affairs* 163(3): 129–147.

Calvocoressi, Peter. 2001. *World Politics 1945–2000*. 8th edition. Essex: Pearson Education Limited.

Carey, Peter, and Pat Walsh. 2008. "The Security Council and East Timor." In *The United Nations Security Council and War: The Evolution of Thought and Practice since 1945*, edited by Vaughan Lowe, Adam Roberts, Jennifer Welsh, and Dominik Zaum, 346–368. Oxford: Oxford University Press.

Chega!. 2008. "Conflict-related deaths in Timor-Leste 1974–1999." Last modified April 2008. http://www.cavr-timorleste.org/en/chegaReport.htm.

Chesterman, Simon. 2007. "East Timor." In *United Nations Interventionism 1991–2004*, edited by Mats Berdal and Sypros Economides, 192–217. Cambridge: Cambridge University Press.

Cortright, David, and George A. Lopez. 2002. *Sanctions and the Search for Security: Challenges to UN Action*. Boulder: Lynne Rienner Publishers.

Cronin, Bruce, and Ian Hurd. 2008. *The UN Security Council and the Politics of International Authority*. Oxon: Routledge.

De Wet, Erika. 2004. *The Chapter VII Powers of the United Nations Security Council*. Portland: Hart Publishing.

Dedring, Juergen. 2008. *The United Nations Security Council in the 1990s: Resurgence and Renewal*. Albany: State University of New York.

Galtung, Johan, Carl G. Jacobsen, and Kai Frithjof Brand-Jacobsen. 2002. *Searching for Peace: The Road to Transcend*. 2nd edition. London: Pluto Press.

Hirst, Paul. 2001. *War and Power in the 21st Century: The State, Military Conflict and the International System*. Cambridge: Polity Press.

Hurd, Ian. 2007. *After Anarchy: Legitimacy and Power in the United Nations Security Council*. Princeton: Princeton University Press.

Kegley, Charles W. Jr., and Gregory Raymond. 1994. *A Multipolar Peace? Great-Power Politics in the Twenty-first Century*. New York: St. Martin's Press.

Malone, David M. 2004. *The UN Security Council: From the Cold War to the 21st Century*. London: Lynne Rienner Publishers.

Manusama, Kenneth. 2006. *The United Nations Security Council in the Post-Cold War Era: Applying the Principle of Legality*. Leiden: Martinus Nijhoff Publishers.

McDougall, Derek. 2007. "'Intervening' in the Neighbourhood: Comparing Australia's Role in East Timor and the Southwest Pacific." *International Journal* 62(4): 867–885.

Paris, Roland. 2001. "Wilson's Ghost: The Faulty Assumptions of Postconflict Peacebuilding." In *Turbulent Peace: The Challenges of Managing International Conflict*, edited by Chester A. Crocker, Fen Osler Hampson, and Pamela Aall, 765–785. Washington: United States Institute of Peace Press.

R. Avgustin, J. 2016. "Analysis of the UN SC authorization of the use of force: Challenging the realistic approach." Ph.D. Diss., University of Ljubljana.

Richmond, Oliver P. 2008. *Peace in International Relations*. New York: Routledge, Taylor & Francis Group.

Roberts, Adam, and Dominik Zaum. 2008. *Selective Security: War and the United Nations Security Council since 1945*. London: Routledge za The International Institute for Strategic Studies.

Roper, John. 1993. *Keeping the Peace in the Post-Cold War Era: Strengthening Multilateral Peacekeeping: a report to the Trilateral Commission*. New York: The Trilateral Commission.

Rothgeb, John M. Jr. 1993. *Defining Power: Influence and Force in the Contemporary International System*. New York: St. Martin's Press.

Rupesinghe, Kumar, and Sanam Naraghu Anderlini. 1998. *Civil Wars, Civil Peace: An Introduction to Conflict Resolution*. London: Pluto Press.

Ryan, Stephen. 2000. *The United Nations and International Politics*. New York: St. Martin's Press.

Schoenbaum, Thomas J. 2006. *International Relations – The Path Not Taken: Using International Law to Promote World Peace and Security*. Cambridge: Cambridge University Press.

Smillie, Ian, and Larry Minear. 2004. *The Charity of Nations: Humanitarian Action in a Calculating World*. Bloomfield: Kumarian Press.

Snow, Donald M., and Eugene Brown. 1996. *The Contours of Power: An Introduction to Contemporary International Relations*. New York: St. Martin's Press.

Strobel, Warren P. 2001. "Information and Conflict." In *Turbulent Peace: The Challenges of Managing International Conflict*, edited by Chester A. Crocker, Fen Osler Hampson, and Pamela Aall, 677–695. Washington: United States Institute of Peace Press.

Taylor, John G. 1994. *Indonesia's Forgotten War: The Hidden History of East Timor*. London: Zed Books.

Thakur, Ramesh. 2006. *The United Nations, Peace and Security: From Collective Security to Responsibility to Protect*. Cambridge: Cambridge University Press.

Trent, John E. 2007. *Modernizing the United Nations System: Civil Society's Role in Moving from International Relations to Global Governance*. Leverkusen Opladen: Barbara Budrich Publishers.

United Nations General Assembly resolutions. Available at: https://www.un.org/en/sections/documents/general-assembly-resolutions/index.html.

United Nations Security Council resolutions. Available at: https://www.un.org/securitycouncil/content/resolutions-0.

Weiss, Thomas G., and Cindy Collins. 2000. *Humanitarian Challenges and Intervention*. 2nd edition. Boulder: Westview Press, Perseus Books Group.

Wheeler, Nicholas J., and Tim Dunne. 2001. "East Timor and the New Humanitarian Interventionism." *International Affairs* 77(4): 805–827.

Woodard, Garry. 1999. "Australia's foreign policy after Timor." *International Journal* 55(1): 1–14.

Ziring, Lawrence, Robert E. Riggs, and Jack C. Plano. 2005. *The United Nations: International Organization and World Politics*. 4th edition. Belmont: Thomson Learning, Wadsworth.

3

The United Nations as both Foe and Friend to Indigenous Peoples and Self-Determination

SHERYL LIGHTFOOT AND DAVID B. MACDONALD

Since the advent of the United Nations (UN) system, Indigenous peoples have been poorly represented, their own self-determining rights and aspirations subsumed by assertions of absolute sovereignty by settler states such as Canada, the United States, Australia, and New Zealand. Settler state governments often perceive Indigenous rights as a threat to state sovereignty and thus seek to 'domesticate' Indigenous nations, preventing them from participating in the UN system as sovereign actors. While the UN has historically been a foe to Indigenous self-determination efforts, changes in recent decades suggest that the UN may be seen increasingly as a friend, providing a base for international coordination, advocacy, and policy change.

This chapter is divided into three parts. The first part explores the challenges and opportunities afforded by the UN system to Indigenous peoples, paying close attention to their exclusion from its creation, and their denial of sovereignty during the 1960s as other colonies gained independence. The second part focuses on how Indigenous peoples have gained influence internationally through the work of the International Indian Treaty Council and other organisations. It also covers how they have attained better recognition of their right to self-determination with the UN Declaration on the Rights of Indigenous Peoples adopted in 2007. Representation, apart from settler states, also takes place at the UN through the Permanent Forum on Indigenous Issues (formed in 2000), the Special Rapporteur on the Rights of Indigenous Peoples (established in 2001), and the Expert Mechanism on the Rights of Indigenous Peoples (2007). The third part balances the potential of the UN for advancing Indigenous sovereignties, while also critiquing the state-centric nature of the system.

The United Nations and the Exclusion of Indigenous Peoples

According to data from the International Work Group for Indigenous Affairs (IWGIA), there are more than 300 million Indigenous peoples in the world, over 5000 distinct peoples living in 72 countries recognised by IWGIA as 'Indigenous'. A precise and objective definition of Indigenous peoples has been exceedingly difficult to achieve due to the vast diversity of Indigenous peoples. After years of heated debate, the UN developed a working definition, centred on three primary elements: 1) a pre-colonial presence in a particular territory, 2) a continuous cultural, linguistic and/or social distinctiveness from the surrounding population, and 3) a self-identification as 'Indigenous' and/or a recognition by other Indigenous groups as 'Indigenous' (Lightfoot 2016).

From its formation in 1945, the UN was, in a sense, a foe to the aspirations of Indigenous peoples for sovereignty because it privileged the sovereignty of many imperial and settler states. This marked a continuation from the former League of Nations, which also favoured Western state sovereignty at the expense of Indigenous peoples and other colonised peoples. A clear example can be seen in the League Mandates, which gave Western powers increased control over Germany's former colonies, without the input from and respect for the Indigenous peoples living there. The League also proved unwilling to help intervene when member states violated their treaties with Indigenous peoples (MacQueen 2018).

Indigenous representatives such as the Tahupōtiki Wiremu Rātana (Ngati Apa and Ngā Wairiki) from Aotearoa New Zealand and Levi General or Deskaheh (Six Nations Haudenosaunee) whose lands are located in present-day Canada, both petitioned the League (Hauptman 2008) to compel the British crown to honour its treaties with Indigenous peoples, only to have the League more or less turn a blind eye (Lightfoot 2016).

After 1945, UN members adopted instruments which advanced their state-centric goals while removing protections for Indigenous peoples. For example, UN members passed the Genocide Convention in 1948, but removed references to cultural genocide which were in the 1947 draft (MacDonald 2019). This was done because many of the policies prohibited in this earlier draft including cultural genocide were actually being performed on Indigenous peoples by settler states. Forced assimilation in residential schools and through fostering and adoption outside of Indigenous communities are two such examples (MacDonald and Gillis 2017).

In the 1960s, UN policies favourable to decolonisation for Africa, Asia, and the Caribbean were deliberately withheld from Indigenous peoples (Anaya 2004). UN General Assembly Resolution 1514 (1960) contained an inherent contradiction: Article 1 asserted the right of all peoples to self-determination, while Article 6 prevented any disruption to 'the national unity and the territorial integrity' of member states. Indigenous peoples were not however considered 'peoples' for the purposes of self-determination and thus had a more difficult time accessing these rights (Anaya 2004). Indigenous peoples were specifically excluded from the UN decolonisation project by the 1960s 'saltwater' or 'blue water' thesis, which asserted that only overseas territories, non-contiguous to the colonial power, were eligible for decolonisation and independent, sovereign statehood (United Nations General Assembly 1960). Thus, as the UN decolonisation project proceeded over the next several decades, Indigenous peoples were left, as Chickasaw legal scholar James (Sa'ke'j) Youngblood Henderson (2008, 34) describes, as 'the unfinished business of decolonisation.'

Indigenous Organisation and International Institutions

While the UN has been largely beholden to state interests, Indigenous peoples have gained influence internationally through the development of networks outside and inside the UN system. Modern activism found its roots during the 1960s and 1970s. While other discriminated groups wanted equal rights, Indigenous peoples wanted both equality and collective recognition as nations, and to regain land stolen by government. The 1960s would herald changes – a sense of collective supratribal Indian identity was appearing as the Indian National Youth Council (established in 1961) grouped members of over 60 different tribes, issuing a Declaration of Indian Purpose (MacDonald 2008). They would eventually stage protest 'fish-ins' – fishing in traditional waters guaranteed by treaty where access was banned by government legislation. Vine Deloria Jr. was the first to use the term 'Red Power' at the 1966 convention of the National Congress of American Indians, which he defined as gaining 'the political and economic power, to run our own lives in our own way' (Quoted in MacDonald 2008). Together with the primarily urban-based American Indian Movement (AIM) (established in 1968) activism began in earnest as the National Indian Brotherhood in Canada was formed in 1968 to represent Status and Treaty Indians, the Inuit Tapirissat was founded in 1971 and organised Inuit in all provinces and territories, and the Grand Council of the Crees was established in 1974 (Lightfoot 2016; Josephy and Nagel 1999).

The 1970s heralded new opportunities for linking local, national, and international efforts through international Indigenous non-governmental organisations (NGOs), such as the International Indian Treaty Council (IITC) (established in 1974), the Inuit Circumpolar Conference (ICC) (established in 1977), and South American and Caribbean regional organisations. During the 1970s, Indigenous peoples came into a number of serious and spectacular conflicts with their respective states.

To name but a few of the most important: the Indian occupation of Alcatraz Island (1969–1971) by 'Indians of All Tribes' – a collective force which claimed 'right of discovery' over the island and offered to buy it for $24 (Johnson, Nagel and Champagne 1997). This is often seen as a cathartic moment for many, a time of solidarity between very different peoples. In Australia, Aboriginal peoples raised their own tent embassy in front of the federal parliament in 1972 while Indigenous groups and police and military confronted one another at Wounded Knee in 1973. In Aotearoa New Zealand, the Brown Power movement formed around the same time, and the Māori also organised the famous 1972 Land March through the country to protest Crown land sales. Canada too saw concerted action against the 1969 White Paper introduced by the federal government to do away with the treaties and treaty rights (Cairns 2011).

One of the early efforts in bringing Indigenous peoples from all parts of the world together seems to have originated with the president of the National Indian Brotherhood in Canada, Chief George Manuel. The first International Conference of Indigenous Peoples was then held in British Columbia, 1975, which resulted in the establishment of the World Council of Indigenous Peoples (WCIP). The WCIP was one of the first Indigenous organisations to pursue observer status in the United Nations, had a secretariat based in Canada, and represented over 60,000,000 Indigenous peoples worldwide; before dissolving in 1996, it was a powerful force for Indigenous peoples, giving its members a concrete experience in international politics (Lightfoot 2016).

Since 1945, the UN has been involved in Indigenous issues through its overall human rights work. Indigenous direct involvement began in 1970 when the Sub-Commission on Prevention of Discrimination and Protection of Minorities (formed by the UN Commission on Human Rights) recommended a study of the problem of discrimination against Indigenous populations, which was carried out by the UN's Special Rapporteur Jose Cobo, who completed it in 1984 (Sanders 1989). The report addressed a wide range of human rights abuses and called on governments to formulate guidelines concerning Indigenous peoples on the basis of respect for their ethnic identity, rights, and freedoms (Sanders 1989).

UN organisations relevant to Indigenous peoples are the Security Council and the General Assembly (there is no hierarchy between these two main bodies), followed by the Economic and Social Council (ECOSOC), the UN Commission on Human Rights (UNCHR), and the Sub-Commission on the Promotion and Protection of Human Rights (Sub-Commission). In 1982, the Working Group on Indigenous Populations (WGIP) was created under the auspices of the Sub-Commission, which provided a new avenue for Indigenous peoples to be heard at the UN level. However, given the low status of working groups within the UN system, recommendations took some time and needed to ascend through many layers before they could be read at the General Assembly level (Charters and Stavenhagen 2009).

The WGIP was instrumental in drafting what later became the Declaration on the Rights of Indigenous Peoples, beginning this process in the early 1980s and producing the first draft in 1993 (Lightfoot 2016). In 2007, the same year that the Declaration was passed by the General Assembly, the structure of the WGIP transformed into the Expert Mechanism on the Rights of Indigenous Peoples (EMRIP). EMRIP is mandated to provide advice and expertise to the Human Rights Council, while also providing recommendations for ways in which the Declaration can be implemented. Seven independent experts, appointed by the Council, communicate regularly and hold an annual meeting on the rights of Indigenous peoples which are appointed by the Human Rights Council (Lightfoot 2016). EMRIP holds an annual meeting which gathers together representatives from Indigenous nations, organisations, state governments, NGOs, civil society organisations, academics, and many others (Assembly of First Nations n.d.; Office of the High Commissioner for Human Rights n.d.a).

Of central importance to Indigenous voices in the UN system is the Permanent Forum, which was established in 2000 as an advisory body to the ECOSOC. It has a mandate to discuss 'Indigenous issues related to economic and social development, culture, the environment, education, health and human rights' (UN Permanent Forum 2019). The Forum holds two-week sessions in New York once a year, usually in May, in which a range of groups participate, including Indigenous organisations, state representatives, UN bodies and organs, inter-governmental organisations and NGOs with ECOSOC consultative status. The first meeting was held in New York in 2002. Sixteen independent experts on Indigenous issues sit as members of the Forum; eight members are nominated by state governments, with election by ECOSOC, while the other eight members are appointed by the President of ECOSOC as regional representatives following wide ranging consultation with Indigenous peoples' organisations.

The Permanent Forum is useful for Indigenous peoples to share information about best practices, common concerns, and strategies to improve Indigenous rights. Much of the Forum's utility lies in its extensive Indigenous Caucus system, a matrix of consultative groups organised according to region or theme. The caucuses are open to all Indigenous delegates and constitute an important locus for meeting, sharing concerns, drafting and promoting joint statements and policy proposals, as well as trying to secure space for specific topics on the Forum agenda (Indigenous Peoples' Centre for Documentation, Research and Information 2012).

In recent decades, the international community has given special attention to the human rights situations of Indigenous peoples. Beginning in 2001 the Commission on Human Rights appointed a Special Rapporteur on the Rights of Indigenous peoples (Charters and Stavenhagen 2009). The Special Rapporteur is tasked with 'promoting good practices, including new laws, government programs, and constructive agreements between Indigenous peoples and states, and to implement international standards' (Office of the High Commissioner for Human Rights n.d.b). They also deliver regular reports including focused country reports on how Indigenous peoples are being treated. The focus is on human rights, and the Special Rapporteur meets with Indigenous peoples and state representatives throughout the countries concerned, paying special attention to cases of human rights violations and abuses (Office of the High Commissioner for Human Rights n.d.b).

These are useful organisations in changing the culture of the UN and also in promoting different norms. Norms are key here, and if we see liberal institutionalism and constructivism as playing important roles in understanding IR, Indigenous mobilisation in the UN system can produce positive effects.

The UN Declaration and the Potential to Enhance Indigenous Sovereignties

As we noted above, the UN Declaration was adopted by the General Assembly in 2007 after several decades of joint drafting and negotiation with over 100 Indigenous organisations. It is a precedent setting document, and as one Indigenous organisation has noted, is: 'the most comprehensive statement of the rights of Indigenous peoples ever developed, giving prominence to collective rights to a degree unprecedented in international human rights law' (Cree Nation Government 2015).

In the end, the Declaration passed the General Assembly with 144 votes in favour, 11 abstentions, and 4 against. The only 4 opposing votes came from Australia, New Zealand, Canada, and the United States, often known as the

CANZUS states (i.e. Canada, Australia, New Zealand, US). The process was instructive: when states face collective pressure from Indigenous peoples asserting their decision-making capacity at the UN, it is hard for them to exclude Indigenous representatives from formal UN procedures. The fact that only four states opposed the Declaration showed it is possible to shame and pressure states as well as negotiate with them to support Indigenous self-determination at UN plenary meetings. In this context, states that support Indigenous rights are more likely to influence the positions of other states by amplifying the voices of Indigenous representatives. The fact that those four recalcitrant states changed position, and that all endorsed the Declaration by the end of 2010, was the result of much domestic lobbying and the operation of a regular procedure for the Special Rapporteur to monitor the plight of Indigenous peoples in particular countries (Lightfoot 2016).

It is no coincidence that the first two of those four countries to renounce their opposition to the Declaration, Australia and New Zealand, were among the first seven countries investigated by Anaya after he took over the role in 2008. Australia announced its support for the Declaration four months before Anaya's scheduled visit in August 2009, while New Zealand announced its support three months before Anaya visited that country in July 2010. For both countries, Anaya's reports (2010; 2011) were critical of entrenched discrimination against Indigenous peoples, though his criticism would have been much stronger if the governments had not changed their policy to support the Declaration.

Prior to the passage of the Declaration in 2007, international human rights law and discourse excluded the two elements that are critical to Indigenous peoples. First, the international human rights regime did not include collective rights to maintain such things as Indigenous culture, language, religion, identity, or their own educational systems in the face of assimilative pressures. Second, Indigenous peoples' self-determination and their collective right to maintain their lands were specifically excluded from the post-World War II UN decolonisation regime by the 'salt water' thesis. These were the 'hard rights' that states, especially settler colonial states, resisted most fiercely and still do. The UN decolonisation era interpretation of self-determination meant independent statehood; the Indigenous rights movement aimed to secure self-determination and land rights for Indigenous nations, with or without statehood, a shift that ultimately requires a global rethinking of how self-determination and land rights can be successfully decoupled from territorial sovereignty.

We can divide rights into 'hard' and 'soft' categories (Lightfoot 2016) to draw out state responses to them. Hard rights strike at some important fundamentals of the existing international system of states: land, territory, sovereignty, and self-determination. These are both difficult to achieve in negotiations and are also a perceived threat to the 'hard core' of the international system, that is, state territorial sovereignty. 'Soft' rights, such as rights to culture, language, education and religion, are collective rights extensions of existing human rights. While recognition and protection of soft rights involves some change to thinking about the inclusion of collective rights, the changes required by states and the UN system are not as fundamental and thus the majority of states accepted them much more readily (Lightfoot 2016).

Global Indigenous politics exerts a particular pressure on the international system to accept a new, non-state-centric interpretation of self-determination, and it therefore is leading a shift in the meaning of self-determination so that it can also be 'interpreted as the right of ...peoples to negotiate freely their political status and representation in the states in which they live' (Daes 1993). The earliest norms literature aimed to show that ideational factors do matter in international politics. Norms, which are understood to mean the behaviour that is appropriate for actors with a certain identity, have been examined in multiple ways. The first studies examined the structure of norms, aiming to counter dominant rationalist understandings of strategic, self-interested international behaviour, show that 'norms matter' (Adler 1997; Kratochwil 1989; Katzenstein 1996; March and Olsen 1998) and demonstrate that states often act in ways that follow a logic of appropriateness (Wendt 1999) based upon inter-subjectively shared norms (Risse 2003; Rues-Smit 1997), rather than maximising their individual benefit. Norms were argued to be constitutive, shaping the interests and identities of state actors (Kowert and Legro 1996; Checkel 1998) yet also regulative and limiting the range of legitimate action (Barkin and Cronin 1994).

Substantial research has been conducted on norm emergence, diffusion, and change, including the 'boomerang effect' of transnational advocacy network campaigns on state behaviour (Keck and Sikkink 1998), the 'spiral model' of human rights norm socialisation (Risse, Ropp and Sikkink 1999), and the study of scope conditions impacting a move from commitment to compliance (Risse, Ropp and Sikkink 2013).

Regarding norms, the nature of global Indigenous rights and politics is dual, operating on the one hand within the existing international order. On the other hand, such rights also serve as a transformational norm vector, helping to move global politics from one norm space to another. The second category of more difficult and problematic Indigenous rights norms and the new ways of doing global politics presented by global Indigenous politics together present challenges to the existing international order. In this the Declaration plays a key role.

Lightfoot's work on the Declaration process (2016) demonstrates several important points about how the final text largely lives up to its original intent, which also represents several important global shifts. It's important to note that the Declaration was always intended to be a set of guidelines for state implementation of Indigenous rights, providing a framework for new Indigenous-state relationships grounded in mutual respect, not state domination. It was also intended to be a persuasive tool, a set of international standards that would be utilised morally and politically in Indigenous rights struggles around the world and, like all human rights declarations, was never intended to be a legally enforceable or legally binding document. As a United Nations declaration and not a convention, it is a political document that became part of the international human rights consensus and its principles are, in some sense, morally binding on all state conduct whether or not an individual state voted for it. Further, the Declaration was always seen as a document of global consensus, not just among UN member states, but also including the active participation of Indigenous peoples in the consensus building process. It is therefore important to understand that this was necessarily a compromise document, ultimately accepted by both states and the Global Indigenous Caucus. As such, Indigenous peoples' right to self-determination (Article 3) sits alongside the right of states to their sovereignty and territorial integrity (Article 46).

The guiding framework of the Declaration therefore expects states to recognise, negotiate and protect a variety of possible self-government or autonomy arrangements for Indigenous peoples, dealing with them as 'peoples', even if not as states. At the same time, it expects Indigenous peoples to negotiate the same with states and not seek secession from or dismemberment of them. However, the UN decolonisation framework remains available for Indigenous peoples who wish to pursue a statehood claim.

The global Indigenous rights regime has forged a set of global changes, with wider implications. First, it seeks the inclusion of a broad set of collective rights into the human rights regime, alongside individual rights, for the first time in history, which Rhiannon Morgan (2011, 2) has described as a radical 'bridging of a paradigmatic gulf' between individual and collective rights. From its earliest beginnings, the Indigenous rights movement has asserted that an exclusively individual rights focus of human rights was insufficient to protect Indigenous peoples. Indigenous peoples also needed protections as collectives, to protect their cultures, societies, and existence as distinct peoples.

Passage of the Declaration by an overwhelming majority of UN member states indicates a fundamental global shift in the human rights regime towards the acceptance of collective rights, although how collective rights will be protected alongside and without disrupting individual rights is not yet entirely clear.

Second, understandings of decolonisation and self-determination have also fundamentally shifted with the passage of the Declaration towards new future constructions. Old colonial doctrines, such as the Doctrine of Discovery and *terra nullius*, have been delegitimised. The Doctrine of Discovery held that European countries who 'discovered' lands inhabited by Indigenous peoples could claim them as part of their own territories and administer and rule over those territories. Indigenous ownership was not recognised in colonial law, and Indigenous peoples were not seen to have rights over their own traditional lands (Miller et al. 2012). *Terra nullius* is a Latin term signifying land without human habitation, meaning that Indigenous peoples were not recognised as humans capable of owning land. This allowed European colonisers to acquire title to the land simply by planting a flag or occupying territory (O'Malley 2014). With the UN Declaration, however, Indigenous peoples' exclusion from the UN decolonisation project has been technically corrected, and Indigenous peoples are now officially included as agents of decolonisation since Indigenous peoples are now specified as enjoying the rights of self-determination equal to all other peoples.

However, the terms and meaning of decolonisation are not as clear as they were in the 1960s era of UN decolonisation, since decolonisation for Indigenous peoples will not, most often, be as independent sovereign states, as Article 46 of the Declaration states:

> Nothing in this declaration may be interpreted as implying for any State, group or person any right to engage in any activity or to perform any act contrary to the Charter of the United Nations or construed as authorising or encouraging any action which would dismember or impair, totally or in part, the territorial integrity or political unity of sovereign and independent States.

The new challenge, therefore, is to imagine and create means of Indigenous self-determination that do not revolve around or rely on state structures. This necessarily involves a decoupling of sovereignty from self-determination, which will eventually impact not only Indigenous peoples, but also all peoples. The wider implication is that self-determination can now mean something other than independent, territorial, sovereign statehood – although the formidable challenge is to create a new meaning that does not result in a diminished, second-class self-determination for Indigenous peoples. The meaning of both self-determination and decolonisation are therefore evolving on the global level and Indigenous rights have an important role to play in the global conversation surrounding that evolution. Due to the intervention of global Indigenous politics, a future imaging of self-determination will likely involve sovereignties that may be plural and multiple, and political relations that are grounded in mutual respect and ongoing negotiated power relations (Lightfoot 2016).

Tracing back to the intellectual tradition of Vine Deloria, Jr. (1979), who argued that the inherent right of self-determination, unbounded by state law and institutions, is a preferable starting point for asserting Indigenous nationhood, political theorist Kevin Bruyneel (2007, 218) promotes an understanding of a 'third space of sovereignty'. Under this conception, Indigenous nations operate neither fully inside nor outside of state structures, which is distinct from both assimilation and secession, and thus offers 'a location of Indigenous postcolonial autonomy that refuses the choices set out by colonial society' (Bruyneel 2007.) Likewise, Audra Simpson (2014) sees the potential for new and better state forms, arguing that various sovereign political orders can be nestled within and between states, although she readily recognises that such an undertaking will involve significant change and problem-solving by all parties.

Third, Indigenous global politics demonstrates that new forms of political relations are possible on the global level. Indigenous global diplomacies have shown that transnational relations can successfully conform to Indigenous ontologies of mutual respect, consensus decision making, non-hierarchical relations, sustainability, and ongoing negotiations. In other words, these 'new' and alternative forms of political practice are actually rooted in very old forms of Indigenous political relations.

Conclusions

As we have sought to demonstrate here, while the UN was originally created to uphold the sovereign power of existing states, and to the detriment of Indigenous peoples, developments since the 1970s point to the UN as a vehicle for Indigenous peoples to organise collectively in favour of their rights. This has included the creation of organisations within the UN system, as well as the passage of the UN Declaration, which is spreading new norms and the potential for what Lightfoot has termed a 'subtle revolution' in how we think about sovereignty, self-determination, and the rights of Indigenous peoples.

This cluster of changes in both the structure and practice of global politics is fundamental enough that Indigenous global politics can be argued to serve as a transformational norm vector, a subtle revolution in global politics. For, if implemented, Indigenous rights involve significant global change not only for Indigenous peoples but change that would alter IR not only in theory, but in practice, thereby pointing the way toward a future beyond the current Westphalian international system, a liberal construction of human rights, and state-centric diplomacies.

References

Adler, Emanuel. 2017. "Seizing the Middle Ground: Constructivism in World Politics." *European Journal of International Relations* 3 (3): 319–363.

Anaya, S. James. 2004. *Indigenous Peoples in International Law.* Oxford: Oxford University Press.

Assembly of First Nations. n.d. "International Advocacy." Accessed November 26, 2018. https://www.afn.ca/policy-sectors/international-advocacy/.

Barkin, J. Samuel, and Bruce Cronin. 1994. "The State and the Nation: Changing Norms and the Rules of Sovereignty in International Relations." *International Organization* 48(1): 107–130.

Bruyneel, Kevin. 2007. *The Third Space of Sovereignty: The Postcolonial Politics of U.S.–Indigenous Relations.* Minneapolis: University of Minnesota Press.

Charters, Claire, and Rodolfo Stavenhagen. 2009. *Making the Declaration Work: The United Nations Declaration on the Rights of Indigenous Peoples.* Copenhagen: International Work Group for Indigenous Affairs.

Cairns, Alan. 2011. *Citizens Plus: Aboriginal Peoples and the Canadian State.* Vancouver: UBC Press.

Checkel, Jeffrey T. 1998. "The Constructivist Turn in International Relations Theory." *World Politics* 50(1): 324–348.

Cree Nation Government. 2015. "United Nations Declaration." Accessed November 26, 2018. http://www.creejustice.ca/index.php/ca/resources/un-declaration.

Daes, Erica-Irene. 1993. *Report of the Working Group on Indigenous Populations on its Eleventh Session*. Geneva: United Nations.

Deloria, Vine. 1979. "Self Determination and the Concept of Sovereignty." In *Economic Development in American Indian Reservations,* edited by Roxanne Dunbar Ortiz, 22–28. Albuquerque: University of New Mexico Development Series 1.

Hauptman, Lawrence M. 2008. *Seven Generations of Iroquois Leadership: The Six Nations since 1800.* Syracuse: Syracuse University Press.

Henderson, James Youngblood. 2008. *Indigenous Diplomacy and the Rights of Peoples: Achieving UN Recognition*. Saskatoon: Purich Publishers.

Indigenous Peoples' Centre for Documentation, Research and Information. 2012. "Fact Sheet on the Permanent Forum on Indigenous Issues." Accessed November 26, 2018. https://www.docip.org/fileadmin/user_upload/Fiche-IP_EN.pdf.

Johnson, Troy R., Joanne Nagel, and Duane Champagne. 1997. *American Indian Activism: Alcatraz to the Longest Walk*. Champaign: University of Illinois Press.

Josephy, Alvin, and Joanne Nagel. 1999. *Red Power: The American Indians' Fight for Freedom.* Lincoln: University of Nebraska Press.

Katzenstein, Peter J. 1996. *The Culture of National Security: Norms and Identity in World Politics*. New York: Columbia University Press.

Keck, Margaret E., and Kathryn Sikkink. 1998. *Activists Beyond Borders: Advocacy Networks in International Politics*. Ithaca: Cornell University Press.

Kowert, Paul, and Jeffrey Legro. 1996. "Norms, Identity, and their Limits: A Theoretical Reprise." In *The Culture of National Security: Norms and Identity in World Politics*, edited by Peter J. Katzenstein, 451–497. New York: Columbia University Press.

Kratochwil, Friedrich. 1989. *Rules, Norms, and Decisions on the Conditions of Practical and Legal Reasoning in International Relations and Domestic Affairs*. Cambridge: Cambridge University Press.

Lightfoot, Sheryl. 2016. *Global Indigenous Politics: A Subtle Revolution.* New York: Routledge.

MacQueen, Norrie. 2018. "The Sins of the Fathers? From League of Nations Mandates to United Nations Peacekeeping." *International Peacekeeping* 25(1): 154–159.

March, James G., and Johan P. Olsen. 1998. "The Institutional Dynamics of International Political Orders." *International Organization* 52(4): 943–969.

MacDonald, David. 2008. *Identity Politics in the Age of Genocide: The Holocaust and Historical Representation.* New York: Routledge.

MacDonald, David, and Jacqueline Gillis. 2017. "Sovereignty, Indigeneity, and Biopower: The Carceral Trajectories of Canada's Forced Removals of Indigenous Children and the Contemporary Prison System." *Sites: New Series* 14(1): 35–55.

MacDonald, David. 2019. The Sleeping Giant Awakens: Genocide, Indian Residential Schools, and the Challenge of Conciliation. Toronto: University of Toronto Press.

Miller, Robert J., Jacinta Ruru, Larissa Behrendt, and Tracey Lindberg. 2012. *Discovering Indigenous Lands: The Doctrine of Discovery in the English Colonies.* Oxford: Oxford University Press.

Morgan, Rhiannon. 2011. *Transforming Law and Institution: Indigenous Peoples, the United Nations and Human Rights.* Burlington: Ashgate.

Office of the High Commissioner for Human Rights. n.d. (a). "Expert Mechanism on the Rights of Indigenous Peoples." Accessed November 26, 2018. https://www.ohchr.org/EN/Issues/IPeoples/EMRIP/Pages/EMRIPIndex.aspx.

Office of the High Commissioner for Human Rights. n.d. (b). "Special Rapporteur on the Rights of Indigenous Peoples." Accessed November 26, 2018. https://www.ohchr.org/en/issues/ipeoples/srindigenouspeoples/pages/sripeoplesindex.aspx.

O'Malley, Vincent. 2014. *Beyond the Imperial Frontier: The Contest for Colonial New Zealand.* Wellington: Bridget Williams Books.

Risse, Thomas. 2003. "The Euro between National and European Identity." *Journal of European Public Policy* 10(4): 487–503.

Risse-Kappen Thomas, Stephen C. Ropp, and Kathryn Sikkink. 1999. *The Power of Human Rights: International Norms and Domestic Change*. Cambridge: Cambridge University Press.

Risse-Kappen, Thomas, Stephen C. Ropp. and Kathryn Sikkink. 2013. *The Persistent Power of Human Rights: From Commitment to Compliance*. Cambridge: Cambridge University Press.

Reus-Smit, Christian. 1997. "The Constitutional Structure of International Society and the Nature of Fundamental Institutions." *International Organization* 51(4): 555–589.

Sanders, Douglas. 1989. "The UN Working Group on Indigenous Populations." *Human Rights Quarterly* 11(3): 406–433.

Simpson, Audra. 2014. *Mohawk Interruptus: Political Life across the Borders of SettlerStates*. Durham: Duke University Press.

United Nations General Assembly. (1960). *Declaration on the Granting of Independence to Colonial Countries and Peoples*. Geneva: United Nations.

United Nations Department of Economic and Social Affairs Indigenous Peoples. 2019. "Permanent Forum." Accessed November 26, 2018. https://www.un.org/development/desa/indigenouspeoples/unpfii-sessions-2.html.

Wendt, Alexander. 1999. *Social Theory of International Politics*. New York: Cambridge University Press.

4

Sustaining Peace and Internal Self-Determination in the UN Perspective

CRISTIANA CARLETTI

The new challenges to prevent, manage and find profitable exit-out solutions from contemporary civil conflicts have called on the International community and the United Nations (UN) system to provide for a renewed promotion of global peace and security for all peoples.

Primary attention in this chapter is firstly put on exploring the new UN vision to cope with critical challenges descending from complex preventive, contextual and post-conflict situations and to improve local knowledge to deal with root causes of conflict towards permanent positive peace and development opportunities. To this purpose the United Nations has recently promoted the new concept of 'sustaining peace' as introduced by both the Report of the Advisory Group of Experts for the 2015 Review of the UN Peacebuilding Architecture and the Report of the High-Level Independent Panel on UN Peace Operations. Its meaning was translated into the UN Security Council (UNSC) and UN General Assembly (UNGA) Resolutions adopted in 2016 (S/RES/2282; A/RES/70/262). According to this relevant approach, also endorsed by the UN Secretary-General (UNSG) (A/72/707–S/2018/43), it is evident that peace and security, human rights and development are interlinked and mutually reinforcing, and that this interlinkage is a profitable means to confirm the crucial importance of self-determination as a key-component of the post-intrastate conflict environment.

Secondly, the relevance of the internal pattern of self-determination is explored. The codification of the right to self-determination in the UN Charter, its legal assertion in the International Human Rights Covenants as well as in the 1960 UN General Assembly Declaration on the Granting of Independence to Colonial Countries and Peoples has extended the legal contents of self-determination by the UN system as a whole. This has steered for the inclusion of the right to take part in public affairs, to have access to the public service of one's own country, to determine a political status and to freely pursue economic, social and cultural development. In last decades the UN has strongly favoured the recognition and implementation of the internal component of the right to self-determination (Pomerance 1982; Rosas 1993; Salmon 1993; Kirgis 1994; Klabbers 2006; Saul 2011a and 2011b; Summers 2013; Demir 2017). This occurred particularly when the UN involved local actors to make the peace process more legitimate and sustainable. Internal self-determination as local ownership should infer the UN intervention for sustaining peace (Donais 2009, 2012; Saul 2011a and 2011b). This impacts the assessment of national needs and capacities, the nature of the country's legal system, the will of concerned parties and – to overcome intra-state crisis – the facilitation of a country-owned and country-led exit built upon the effective use of local capacities and institutions. But, in recent times, a new interpretation of the principle of self-determination, the so called hybrid self-determination (Richmond 2009; Weller 2009; Mac Ginty 2010; Senaratne 2013; Bell 2016), has been investigated due to its proved relevance in overcoming past failures and to redefine a new constitutional setting along the lines of the peace agreement's contents.

In the last part of the chapter an alternative reading of the set of peace agreement models that entered into force from 2000 to 2018 is proposed to investigate the feasibility of hybrid self-determination and its ability to strengthen the internal component of this principle as a core target of the post-conflict sustaining peace process promoted and guided under UN leadership. Analysis of some specific provisions of selected peace agreements already in force and the role of the UN in facilitating their negotiation and helpful implementation is provided to demonstrate how much the internal self-determination/hybrid self-determination component could positively influence post-conflict sustaining peace- and nation-building processes.

The Concept of Sustaining Peace: A New UN Approach to Dealing with Conflict Issues

The issue of conflict in the 21st century is a complex matter. The common root causes that typified the most part of civil wars in the late 1990s and that were identified also since the beginning of the present century are represented by fragile institutional settings (Hannum 1990; O'Connell 1992; Werner 2001; Paris 2004).

Partially unexpected contingency of dynamics has played a significant role in adding more complexity to contemporary conflicts, thus contributing to a higher fragmented idea of traditional drivers and of a right approach to positively deal with them. This has incentivised emerging forms of violence and extremism (Chen 1991; Chadwick 1996; Hilpold 2017) as well as new populist movements which aimed at excluding ethnic, religious and cultural minorities to be politically treated and controlled, avoiding any form of revenge for joint public governance. These minorities have further suffered from a concrete marginalisation from access to and exploitation of economic and environmental resources (Thornberry 1989, 1993; Hannum 1991; Green 1995). A higher percentage of domestic conflicts and related relapses have been produced by weak administration of public resources such as land and water, which puts at risk the stability of the concerned areas and becomes a strong factor in regional and local conflicts. Further, the high-level involvement of vulnerable and disadvantaged peoples in criminal activity has translated into intractable rebel movements (Tomuschat 1992; Quinn 2007; Summers 2007; Sriram 2008). The emergency has become a permanent out-of-law setting where the absence of a robust and credible institutional actor has undermined the traditional concept of state sovereignty at the core of the international legal order.

This has prompted reflection on the relevance of international players, the UN system in particular being confronted with the critical ability of national authorities to prevent and, if it is the case, to manage the new features of contemporary conflicts. Following the collapse or prolonged absence of a central government in a failed state, the traditional international system has also considered the opportunity to assume a different position (Lund 2003; Tschirgi 2004; Chetail 2009). In this context the UN has tried to adapt its original statutory mandate into 'sustaining peace', so far expanding it to become flexible enough to encompass the promotion and protection of human rights. This has supported the principle of self-determination to be considered as an essential prerequisite to prevent and manage contemporary conflicts.

From the UN Agenda for Peace to the Reform of the UN Peacebuilding Architecture

Since the first revision of the UN approach to deal with international peace and security at the beginning of the 1990s, as illustrated by the UNSG in 1992 in its *Agenda for Peace* (A/47/277- S/24111), progressive deterioration of nation-state contexts was tackled through the establishment and the gradual improvement of the following three entities: the Peacebuilding Commission (PBC), the Peacebuilding Fund and the Peacebuilding Support Office.

A different operational approach was provided in the *Supplement to an Agenda*, adopted in 2001 by the UNSC (S/PRST/2001/5), where peacebuilding was considered a relevant complement to the first two UN actions, and followed by the creation of the UNSG Advisory Group of Experts on the 2015 Review of the United Nations Peacebuilding Architecture (A/69/968-S/2015/490; A/64/868 – S/2020/393). This intervention has been aimed at giving tailored assistance to prevent and solve intra-state conflicts, i.e. to sustaining peace with the active participation of populations directly affected by intra-state conflicts as a one-off precondition (Bell 2017a and 2017b).

The UN 'Sustaining Peace' Approach: The Conceptual Analysis and its Operational Practicability

The UN 'sustaining peace' approach is aimed at managing peace embracing prevention, handling exit out and post-conflict strategies. Sustaining peace means to restore dialogue and consultation with local communities, to rely on the credibility and support from public and private individuals and collective stakeholders, to frame new settings and to encompass critical root causes and dynamics that have contributed to fuel the conflict" (A/72/707–S/2018/43).

The inclusive component of the 'sustaining peace' approach is based on the trust of national authorities and domestic actors' categories: minorities, representatives of vulnerable individuals, the private sector, civil society, under-represented groups or peoples. It has the 'broaden ownership' concept at its core: it means to ensure a high-intensity participatory approach from the first stage of the post-conflict process; at the same time it lets non-institutional counterparts give their contribution in the definition of policies, actions, programmes and projects, in the implementation of predetermined measures, and in the monitoring and evaluation of results, to avoid any form of re-collapse into the conflict (Brown and Grävingholt 2011; de Coning 2016).

The 'sustaining peace' approach should ensure the active participation of peoples, also encompassing vulnerable individuals that are the most likely to be excluded from contributing to the creation of a positive post-conflict setting. From one side this has meant the reinforcement of the central role of the organisation in conveying the maximum engagement of international stakeholders and the taking of root causes, basic needs, dynamics of the country-situation into consideration. When the UN has not reserved specific attention to the principle of self-determination, only an in-depth preliminary analysis of all political and economic drivers has been proved as effective enough in the short, medium and long term. To this goal the UN Headquarters are requested to work in close cooperation with local bodies to perform the common tasks for consolidating peace in the exit-out strategies and in contributing to rebuild the nation-state moving from the self-determination vision. Particularly, the UNSG has played and plays nowadays a key role, directly or through his representatives, to get into contact and dialogue with national public and private stakeholders. The common aim has been to define a political roadmap in order to overcome emergency needs and to implement a series of cross-cutting measures impacting the three pillars of the organisation – i.e. international peace and security, development and human rights – to achieve concretely a 'sustaining peace'.

On the other side, the new UN approach has evidently resulted in adjusting the original peace operations' substantial and procedural fundamentals. The recent proposal of the High-Level Independent Panel on Peace Operations on this point has been based on the elaboration of a package of sequenced actions with few and clear priorities and operational tasks: they should all respond to primary needs of the affected population and their need to restart by its own self-determination.

The 'sustaining peace' approach will work also in a preventive perspective to avoid any form of short-term re-collapse into the conflict but also to update the guiding principles of the UN peace interventions. As reminded by the UNSG in his last report, conflict prevention and mediation are core-tools that must be re-prioritised to respond to the political and social dynamics of national and local communities at risk. This will lead to the primacy of political solutions in relation to existing or potential conflicts; indeed, political solutions have to be considered as a relevant and complementary tool in association with the military component of UN peace operations and apart from any direct link to the self-determination principle.

In other words, the transition from peace-making to peacekeeping and peacebuilding calls primarily for a new and stronger partnership among all the national and international concerned stakeholders, preserving enough flexibility to deal with cross-cutting problems at the normative and operational level.

To sum up, investing in 'sustaining peace' encompasses the international and national actors' will to be fully committed for a long-term implementation of a peace agreement. This engagement goes along the lines of a virtuous cycle. It starts from preventing conflicts before their escalation; it passes through the management of violent conflicts by using political tools and achieving good compromises by mediation; and it is completed when good governance, rule of law, democracy, human rights protection and internal self-determination are really guaranteed in a positive peace setting.

Internal Self-Determination Impacting the Substantial Elements of Peace Agreements: For a New Challenging Peace Sustaining Vision

The original legal definition of the principle of self-determination was strictly linked to the notion of the nation-state emerging in the 1960s decolonisation process. It was claimed by populations in order to change their status of independence as well as to confirm the relevance of the concept of territorial integrity (Cassese 1981 and 1995; Tomuschat 1993; Koskenniemi 1994).

Beyond this historical context the opportunity to expand the aforementioned principle by giving it a comprehensive legal relevance was endorsed by the UN system in the 1970s: in line with articles 1 and 2 of the UN Charter, the common article 1 of the International Covenant on Civil and Political Rights and International Covenant on Economic, Social and Cultural Rights provided that "all peoples have the right to self-determination [...] to freely determine their political status and freely pursue their economic, social and cultural development".

On one side the chance for a wider interpretation was frustrated and limited to internal struggles against the former or new governmental authorities in order to achieve the full enjoyment of fundamental rights via a secessionist-based process (Moore 1998; Walter et al. 2014). On the other side the individual and collective commitment to accomplish self-government has required the cross-examination of the concept of territorial integrity; its application has been critically proved when it was related to secessionist claims from populations or minorities as relevant component of the same population (Crawford 2001).

To overcome these inconsistencies with the aim to highlight the internal component of the principle of self-determination, two proposals were formulated by the best doctrine which have a common background: the negotiation of peace agreements following an intra-state conflict, whereas the UN has often played a relevant and positive role also for the recognition and the concrete respect of the principle itself.

Firstly, the principle has been considered as a procedural right to be enjoyed by the peoples who have a high interest in participating in decision-making processes directly affecting them. This has encompassed not only the rights related to direct democracy in a post-conflict setting but also the regular participation in all decisions concerning the protection and promotion of civil, political, economic, social and cultural rights (Klabbers 2006).

Subsequently, a different meaning of the principle of sovereignty has been used to confirm the internal legitimacy and the external independence of a nation-state. As to the former, the development of international law has contributed for an advanced relevance of the principle of self-determination. It was defined as a core right to be fulfilled at the domestic level in favour of individuals and peoples. And it was envisaged as a core obligation imposed on governmental authorities: the duty to ensure the exercise of democratic rights; participation in electoral processes which freely determine the political status of the nation-state; the protection of minority rights; and the progressive accomplishment of economic, social and cultural rights. The latter observation deserves specific attention and should be explored in relation to positive peace, following negotiation and the entering into force of a peace agreement, in the view of avoiding a re-collapse into intra-state conflict and of promoting the new UN model of 'sustaining peace'.

In general terms the peace agreement – embracing the different legal patterns of the cease-fire agreement, the framework agreement and the agreement for the implementation of legal commitments at the national level – is the tool that lets the institutional and non-institutional counterparts of a conflict compose their contrasts according to primary political, economic and social interests (Bell 2006; Carletti 2008).

There are three main stages where the principle of self-determination could emerge and be treated in order to contribute to a lasting peace (Bell 2008). At the first stage, the aim is to redefine the nation-state setting: it means to give new emphasis to the legitimacy of the governmental system at the central and local levels as well as to amend or include key constitutional principles for its functioning – i.e. democracy, rule of law, human rights, inclusiveness and participation in decision-making processes (Aroussi and Vanderginste 2013; Kaldor 2016). Then, according to the principle of territorial integrity and full sovereignty of the nation-state, a complete institutional framework should be built into central governance bodies and mechanisms and disaggregated territorial powers. The latter are useful to take into account the demand for participation from those ones vindicating the self-determination principle within a non-violent power disaggregation process (McWhinney 2007). The third stage is represented by the recognition of an external support: it is represented by the external power temporarily dislocated from the national territory to uphold the 'sustaining peace' process and to reinforce the linkage between the renewed legitimate institutional setting and the population in the implementation of the peace agreement (Barnett and Zürcher 2009; Chandler 2015).

This approach, as mentioned above could be extremely relevant to avoid any secessionist movement. This fear could be managed only if the international presence in domestic governance management is really temporary and if it is aimed at accommodating the different but complementary interests of the groups composing the entire population. So far, the exercise of national sovereignty is not completely ascribed to one internal or external power but is shared between them. It is dislocated to facilitate the relationship among political and social competitors and it might offer a new interpretation of the principle of self-determination (so called 'hybrid self-determination') to overcome past failures and to redefine a new constitutional setting along the lines of the peace agreement's contents (Boege et al. 2008; Mac Ginty 2010 and 2011; Mac Ginty and Richmond 2015).

The Hybrid Self-Determination: Substantial and Procedural Features

The hybrid self-determination concept moves from the need to translate its international content into a constitutionalising process to endorse the peace agreements provisions at the post-conflict domestic level (Bell and Zulueta-Fuelscher 2016). The success of this process is driven by the full recognition of the aforementioned concept both in substantive and procedural terms and the UN contribution has proved to be nearly effective to this scope.

The substantial content is acknowledged as the right to an effective and fair participation to institutions and to public decision-making mechanisms. If the normative relevance of the principle of self-determination is out of the question at the international level and within the UN legal framework, the compromise between its core elements and the principle of territorial integrity and full sovereignty is yet questionable. It means that the principle, to be accepted and to support the revitalisation of the legitimacy of the constitutional power in a post-conflict situation, should be conceived as hybrid and facilitated by external actors – e.g. the UN – into the new domestic setting (Fox and Roth 2000). The latter are required to work to develop new internal legal standards consistent with international law (Kymlicka 2007; Knop 2008; Valadez 2018). In this sense the hybridity is considered not an obstacle but a driver substantially – and also linguistically – apt to reconcile opposing visions and interests into a composite and appreciable nation-state setting. Indeed, it grants representation and participation as a precondition of the relationship between the government and its population. In other terms, hybridity impacts a common legal standards baseline that is strong and weak at the same time. Under UN leadership the constitutional contents have been included in the peace agreement so as to overcome negative violent reactions from populations; at the same time the institutional framework has been soft-contractualised as the optimal solution for the entire community (Sapiano et al. 2016).

The last observation reminds of the procedural component of the concept that is enshrined in the right to freely express opinions and be seriously heard in the negotiation of the peace agreement and its full implementation. Though the UN is tentative in granting this precondition throughout the post-conflict process, it is a matter of fact that the procedural component has a complex and dynamic feature. The fair and active participation for the redefinition of the nation-state, the disaggregation and the dislocation of power appear as a proper right: it should be completed by the definition of a multiple set of governance issues to be negotiated and implemented at the national level – i.e. power levels, reform of the judiciary, management of the military and police forces, human rights domestic machinery. These institutional arrangements are quite relevant per se but not enough valid in their own substance. The hybridity of self-determination is also a dynamic process that should be tested regularly and, if it is the case, to be amended to ensure the political and social inclusiveness of populations in legitimating the institutional powers. In other terms hybridity is placed among the notions of representative and participatory democracy: the first is certified by the strong but circumstanced relation between governmental bodies and their electors; the latter is enshrined in the exercise of the citizenry, in its high qualitative level and in the preservation of a factual inclusiveness into the governance system as a whole beyond the electoral process. Really power-sharing principles and mechanisms for joint governance responsibility let the peace agreement inform the constitutionalising process based on an equal and fair recognition of individual and collective participatory rights.

Peace Agreement Models Including Hybrid Self-determination as a Core Target of the Post-conflict Sustaining Peace Process

An alternative reading of the set of peace agreement models that entered into force from 2000 to 2018 is here proposed to investigate the feasibility of the hybrid self-determination and its impact to strengthen the internal component as a core target of the post-conflict sustaining peace process (Melandri 2015). At the same time the role and action of the UN in the cases reported below could confirm the relevance of this target, as endorsed, to positively and concretely help concerned countries deal with the criticalities arising from the post-conflict setting.

As it concerns intra-state conflicts aimed at claiming secessionist targets hybrid self-determination has led to the following three results: the establishment of a new state identity; the recognition of groups previously excluded from democratic participation; a constitutional and institutional reform encompassing basic standards of representative and participatory democracy. At the same time the disaggregation of powers has entailed autonomous solutions, granting a higher level of protection of human rights, equality rights and political and social inclusiveness. Finally, the dislocation of powers has deserved a temporary contribution from international actors, with a gradual governance devolution and the decision to postpone territorial integrity and constitutional setting solutions at a later stage. One example could be mentioned in such contexts – the Papua New Guinea Bougainville Peace Agreement (S/2001/988).

In Papua New Guinea the hybrid nature of the principle of self-determination has been introduced since the adoption of the draft basic agreement of 24 December 1998. The agreement aimed at establishing the new governmental framework moving from the formal recognition of the self-determination principle in a proper act – in this case a resolution was explicitly mentioned – in order to regulate the matter and the manner for implementing it. At the same time the hybridity was encompassed by the availability of options that could be adopted in view of 'developing a peaceful outcome to the negotiations'. Indeed in the following step pursuing the drafting and formal approval of the Bougainville Peace Agreement, on 30 August 2001, a mutual compromise was introduced: it reflected the hybrid idea of self-determination, as endorsed in the autonomy objectives jointly accepted by the contracting parties – i.e. the National Government and the Bougainville Government. Assuming the sovereignty of Papua New Guinea, the arrangements provided by the aforementioned Peace Agreement confirm the Bougainville identity but the promotion of fruitful relationships with 'the rest of Papua New Guinea'. Moreover a multifaceted purpose (S/2001/988) was pursued to gain a double and mutually effective approach for both contracting parties: to recognise their formal and functional roles and to work together to achieve the same objective, i.e. the unity and prosperity of Papua New Guinea (Peace Agreement Access Tool 1998).

The UN's helpful and coherent intervention in Papua New Guinea has had a twofold objective which reminds of the proper hybrid nature of the self-determination principle. From one side the reinforcement of the inclusive approach was pursued in relation to governmental authorities and civil society representatives in order to improve a democratic, transparent and accountable governance. On the other side a targeted assistance to local authorities of the Autonomous Region of Bougainville was sought. This meant to prevent any form of violence attempting the political, economic and social security and personal safety of peoples, and to support the local parliament in facilitating the exchange of information, and active participation of the people of Bougainville towards the next referendum, scheduled for 2019.

In relation to solutions for intra-state conflicts grounded on historical ethnic struggles, the opportunity for a re-definition of the status of the nation-state is introduced. This tentative was explored by referring to multiple factors enabling alternative solutions inspired by the utmost inclusive approach of minorities. Among the most relevant factors, the following are worth mentioning; full recognition of their fundamental rights, respect of the principle of equality, promotion of dialogue and mutual understanding, reinforcement of democracy, rule of law and good governance. The power has been disaggregated providing for concrete and balanced institutional participation at the central and local levels. The dislocation of power has been granted through a progressive translation of competences from international to domestic bodies. This has meant to negotiate firstly a cease-fire agreement; then to promote a process aimed at ensuring the gradual establishment of a constitutional and legislative framework under the monitoring of international observers; and finally the compilation of a definitive constitutional text to be confirmed by referendum as the precondition for democratic elections. In such contexts the hybrid self-determination has been put at risk to be partially accomplished, due to the predominant transitional setting waiting for an agreed consolidated alternative from all the contenders (Bell and Pospisil 2017). A relevant example of Sri Lanka could be mentioned in this scope.

Here the hybrid nature of the self-determination principle emerged during peace talks carried out by the Government of Sri Lanka and the Liberation Tigers of Tamil Eelam. On the occasion of the release of the Oslo Communique on 5 December 2002 the need to explore a balanced solution was reported. It encompassed the internal self-determination as well as the establishment of a governance federal option within a united country. In the following debate promoted in 2003 concerning the human rights component – to be safeguarded as a key factor for the success of the peace process – the principle was reaffirmed as the precondition for the enjoyment of collective rights. In the last stage, i.e. the Agreed Statement adopted by the parties on 21 March 2003, internal self-determination was considered the core prerequisite to the development of a federal system 'within a united, federal Sri Lanka' by introducing the preliminary organic setting to launch and manage this process (Peace Agreement Access Tool 2002; Peace Agreement Access Tool 2003a; Peace Agreement Access Tool 2003b).

The achievement of a condition of positive peace within the country has facilitated the UN action to sustain the National Unity Government in the peacebuilding and national reconciliation process launched in 2009. A concrete support was particularly ensured in 2015 through financial support granted by the UN Peacebuilding Support Office (by the so called Peacebuilding Fund – Peacebuilding and Recovery Facility); also the release of technical assistance in developing a Peacebuilding Priority Plan was provided, anticipated by an ad hoc assessment and based on four priority areas: Transitional Justice, Reconciliation, Good Governance, and

Resettlement and Durable Solutions. The Plan was finalised in close consultation with civil society in June 2016 for a three year cycle. UN assistance concerning the good governance area was inspired by the hybridity of the self-determination principle for the accomplishment of a 'political solution'. It encompassed the opportunity for a merged territorial unit covering the Northern and Eastern Provinces of the country – where reluctant Muslim and Sinhalese communities lived – and the extended self-administration, through the power devolution in favour of the Tamil people. This approach, which could be considered as having had a positive impact until now, is under implementation to avoid any relapse into ethnic conflict and to catch the present challenges for going forward.

Intra-state conflicts, which are basically characterised to replace institutional authoritarian systems and are partially intended to stress the relevance of the principle of self-determination, claim the need to reaffirm the nation-state's key values and democratic standards. As for the redefinition of the state, a comprehensive renewed commitment to the protection of human rights, inclusiveness and democratic accountability is the prerequisite for a stronger linkage between institutions and peoples to reinforce the sovereign legitimacy of the former over the latter. The disaggregation of powers is represented by the reconfiguration of the political parties' setting: it involves all contenders – former military parties and civil society organisations – in democratic elections as well as in participatory decision-making processes other than the electoral ones. The power has been also dislocated in favour of international actors that were requested to facilitate the best implementation of peace agreements.

The most exemplificative case is the one of Nepal. Here the agreement reached between the Government Talks Team, including the basic Seven Political Parties, and the Federal Limbuwan State Council, signed on 19 March 2008, was based upon a balanced compromise to avoid any form of government inspired by feudalist and strongly centralised patterns and to involve all peoples for a unitary state model well beyond the original demand for a Limbuwan Autonomous State. This encompassed a common state rebuilding commitment 'along with the right to self-determination', joined with the 'right to ethnic identity and autonomy', according to the former historical context and the will of creating a 'peaceful, prosperous and modern new Nepal'. So far the hybrid self-determination rested on the intention to establish a federal democratic republic – the so called 'national main-streaming' – and to preserve the ethnical components and the respective autonomies of the Nepalese peoples (Agreement Reached between the Government Talks Team comprising Seven Political Parties and the Federal Limbuwan State Council 2008).

To achieve this objective the UN established in 2007 the United Nations Mission in Nepal (UNMIN), with a progressively renewed, peculiarly light military mandate to monitor and assess the implementation of the peace agreement in the political and governance perspective. The risk of deterioration of the situation and reiterated tensions led UNMIN to support the conflicting parties: on 13 September 2010 the Nepalese Government and the UCPN-Maoist party signed a new agreement in which they pledged to take up the remaining tasks of the peace process to complete them by 14 January 2011. It is a matter of fact that the preliminary and latter results from the UN contribution clearly diverge as for the peace process. Different analytical positions were expressed about the successful UN assistance for the stabilisation of the domestic framework and the relevance of the principle of hybrid self-determination, for the implementation of peacebuilding activities and in the view of preventing any re-collapse into the war. The UN intervention was probably inspired by the tentative of hybridisation of the principle of self-determination; the UN took into account the institutional centralisation and the exclusion of local powers for multiple and complementary root causes such as caste, ethnicity, religion, gender. However, the international early military and political engagement was shifted into a lower-intensity capacity to facilitate the dialogue among conflicting parties: this left ultimately to local power the control over the peace consolidation towards a federalist solution. This means that the hybrid self-determination principle whenever managed by local elites, marginally supported by international actors, could turn into new tensions and violence. This occurred firstly in 2013 with the dissolution of the Constituent Assembly, then with heavy protests recorded since September 2015 against the constitution-making process. Finally, with an ongoing silent opposition by the Joint Democratic Madhesi Front was recorded for a federalist option which is embedded in the broader institutional reform process and that could fuel the discriminatory component of the forthcoming governance system.

Some Concluding Observations

The inclusion of the principle of hybrid self-determination in peace agreements could be a relevant tool to support the new UN 'sustaining peace' model. As proposed by the best doctrine before the launch of the UN revitalisation of the peace-building architecture, there are four nuanced outcomes to this scope (Bell 2008).

Within a potential first setting the peace law could be used to provide for an alternative and creative solution: it could be based on a 'disaggregation of concepts of statehood, territory, peoples and nationalities' that inform the ongoing process of defining the relationship among international legal order, statehood, nationhood, principles of self-determination, territorial integrity and sovereignty. This background gives the peace agreement a transitional and constitutional value to resume all the claims of contenders in a 'complex multinational post-sovereign state'. In this framework the UN leadership could positively contribute to this scope through the reinforcement of the legal framework and the empowerment of the participatory approach, as occurred in some circumstances in previous years.

In a more creative manner peace agreements including the hybrid self-determination component could be considered as the right tool to cope with co-factors that had led to the complete dysfunctionality of the state. Here the constitutional requirements enshrined in the peace agreement are used to move from the international legal order towards the rebuilding of nationhood, ensuring a full engagement of all the contenders. Within this context the UN could only play a strong but preliminary role; the organisation leaves the pave for a proper translation of the principle under reference into the new domestic legal framework, avoiding a useless and counterproductive perpetuity of its presence on the field.

The impact of peace agreements including a hybrid self-determination component could be evaluated in a stricter manner, taking into consideration only the immediate results of the transitional process to liberal democracy. Here te hybridity entails a partial short-time result represented by the reinforcement of human rights protections and the planning and performing of elections. This preliminary outcome is remarked as an expected technical result to be forcibly completed by further steps in the transitional process leading the international legal order to be superseded by the domestic constitutional order. Along this line it could only be demanded that the UN monitor the full respect of international human rights law and recommend its implementation by nation-building actors.

The last option to use the peace agreement including a hybrid self-determination component is the most conservative. Due to existing and not yet solved conflicts between contenders, the real impact of the peace agreement is limited. Neither could it support the transitional powers process – maintained by the older governmental authorities – nor could it provide for a comprehensive transformation of the statehood which responds to the basics of liberal democracy. Along these circumstances the same substantial and formal features of peace agreements are not fluid and flexible enough to encourage a positive transitional process. The narrative could only lead to review of the institutional setting without a real contribution from below. The UN has experienced several cases where its contribution has not enabled the contenders to really exit out from the conflict. There is also, however, a worst-case scenario: the preservation of the older statehood. It could mean that the provisions of the peace agreement are so hybrid to induce to destroy the self-determination concept and to facilitate the adoption of a new imperialist set of policies and practices. In other terms the institutional setting is not only preserved but also aims to grant less independence and less equality and to strengthen the exclusion of the underrepresented who fight for the creation of a new liberalist nationhood framework. These are the cases where the UN has been mostly criticised for the powerlessness to hold its statutory mandate and the inactivity to prevent, restore and maintain international peace and security. Critics have been summarised in pushing for a comprehensive reform of the first pillar of the organisation in favour of the elaboration of the new concept of 'sustaining peace'.

All the above-mentioned options to read the peace agreement's hybrid self-determination component demonstrate how international and national actors could impact the establishment of a post-intrastate conflict environment domestically. In doing so to maintain international peace and security, to protect human rights and to promote human development, 'sustaining peace' could be properly guaranteed. For the UN this challenge could be considered a concrete tool for testing the need for a renewed reading of its role and mandate to tackle contemporary conflicts and to strengthen international human rights law and the principle of self-determination.

References

Agreement Reached between the Government Talks Team comprising Seven Political Parties and the Federal Limbuwan State Council. 2008. In *From Conflict to Peace in Nepal: Peace Agreements 2005–10*, edited by Izumi Wakagawa, Prawash Gautam, and Anil Shrestha, 117–119. Kathmandu: Asian Study Center for Peace & Conflict Transformation.
https://www.peaceagreements.org/masterdocument/1751.

Aroussi, Sahla and Stef Vandeginste. 2013. "When Interests Meet Norms: The Relevance of Human Rights for Peace and Power-Sharing." *The International Journal of Human Rights* 17: 183–203.

Barnett, Michael and Christoph Zürcher2009. "The Peacebuilder's Contract: How External Statebuilding Reinforces Weak Statehood." In *The Dilemmas of Statebuilding: Confronting the Contradictions of Postwar Peace Operations*, edited by Roland Paris and Timothy D. Sisk, 25–32. New York: Routledge.

Bell, Christine. 2006. "Peace Agreements: Their Nature and Legal Status." *American Journal of International Law* 100: 373–412.

Bell, Christine. 2008. *On the Law of Peace. Peace Agreements and the Lex Pacificatoria.* Oxford: Oxford University Press.

Bell, Christine. 2016. "Political Settlement and the New Logic of Hybrid Self-determination." In *New Logics in the Relations of Legal Orders*, edited by H. Patrick Glenn and Lionel D. Smith, 129–161. Cambridge: Cambridge University Press.

Bell, Christine. 2017a. "Introduction: Bargaining on constitutions – Political settlements and constitutional state-building." *Global Constitutionalism* 6: 13–32.

Bell, Christine. 2017b. "Peace settlements and Human Rights: A Post Cold-War circular history." *Journal of Human Rights Practice* 9: 358–378.

Bell, Christine and Kimana Zulueta-Fuelscher. 2016. *Sequencing Peace Agreements and Constitutions in the Political Settlement Process.* Stockholm: International Institute for Democracy and Electoral Assistance.

Bell, Christine and Jan Pospisil. 2017. "Navigating inclusion in transitions from conflict: The formalised political unsettlement." *Journal of International Development* 29: 576–593.

Boege, Volker, Anne Brown, Kevin Clements, and Anna Nolan. 2008. *"On Hybrid Political Orders and Emerging States: State Formation in the Context of 'Fragility'".* Handbook Dialogue 8, 2–21. Berlin: Berghof Foundation. https://www.berghof-foundation.org/fileadmin/redaktion/Publications/Handbook/Articles/boege_etal_handbook.pdf.

Brown, Stephen and Jörn Grävingholt. 2011. *From Power Struggles to Sustainable Peace: Understanding Political Settlements.* Paris: Organisation for Economic Co-operation and Development (OECD).

Carletti, Cristiana. 2008. *Gli accordi di pacificazione nel diritto internazionale.* Torino: Giappichelli Editore.

Cassese, Antonio 1981. "The Self-Determination of Peoples." In *The International Bill of Rights*, edited by Louis Henkin, 92–113. New York: Columbia University Press.

Cassese, Antonio. 1995. *Self-Determination of Peoples: A Legal Reappraisal*. Cambridge: Cambridge University Press.

Chadwick, Elizabeth. 1996. *Self-Determination, Terrorism, and the International Humanitarian Law of Armed Conflict*. The Hague: Martinus Nijhoff Publishers.

Chandler, David. 2015. "Reconceptualizing international intervention: statebuilding, 'organic processes' and the limits of causal knowledge." *Journal of Intervention and Statebuilding* 9: 70–88.

Chen, Lung-Chu. 1991."Self-Determination and World Public Order." *Notre Dame Law Review* 66: 1287–1297.

Chetail, Vincent. 2009. *Post-Conflict Peacebuilding: A Lexicon*. Oxford: Oxford University Press.

Crawford, James. 2001. "The Right of Self-Determination in International Law: Its Development and Future." In *People's Rights*, edited by Philip Alston, 7–68. Oxford: Oxford University Press.

de Coning, Cedric. 2016. "From peacebuilding to sustaining peace: implications of complexity for resilience and sustainability. Resilience: International Policies." *Practices and Discourses* 4: 166–181.

Demir, Ebru. 2017. "The right to internal self-determination in peacebuilding processes: a reinterpretation of the concept of local ownership from a legal perspective." *Age of Human Rights* 8: 18–48.

Donais, Timothy. 2009. "Inclusion or Exclusion? Local ownership and Security Sector Reform." *Studies in Social Justice* 3: 117–131.

Donais, Timothy. 2012. *Peacebuilding and Local Ownership: Post-conflict Consensus Building*. London: Routledge.

Fox, Gregory H. 1995. "Self-Determination in the Post-Cold War Era: A New Internal Focus?" *Michigan Journal of International Law* 16: 733–781.

Fox, Gregory H. and Brad R. Roth. 2000. *Democratic Governance and International Law*. Cambridge: Cambridge University Press.

General Assembly Resolution 47/277, *An Agenda for Peace: Preventive diplomacy, peacemaking and peace-keeping report of the Secretary General*, A/47/277- S/24111 (17 June 1992), available from https://undocs.org/A/RES/47/277.

General Assembly Resolution 70/262, *Review of the United Nations peacebuilding architecture*, A/RES/70/262 (27 April 2016), available from undocs.org/en/A/RES/70/262.

Green, Leslie. 1995. "Internal Minorities and their Rights." In *Group Rights*, edited by Judith Baker, 257–272. Toronto: University of Toronto Press.

Hannum, Hurst. 1990. *Autonomy, Sovereignty, and Self-Determination. The Accommodation of Conflicting Rights*. Philadelphia: University of Pennsylvania Press.

Hannum, Hurst. 1991. "Contemporary Developments in the International Protection of the Rights of Minorities." *Notre Dame Law Review* 66: 1431–1448.

Hilpold, Peter. 2017. "Self-determination and Autonomy: Between Secession and Internal Self-determination." *International Journal on Minority and Group Rights* 24: 302–335.

International Covenant on Civil and Political Rights, New York, 19 December 1966, *United Nations Treaty Series*, vol. 999, p. I-14668, available from https://treaties.un.org/doc/publication/unts/volume%20999/volume-999-i-14668-english.pdf.

International Covenant on Economic, Social and Cultural Rights, New York, 19 December1966, *United Nations Treaty Series*, vol. 993, p. 3, available from https://treaties.un.org/doc/Publication/UNTS/Volume%20993/v993.pdf.

Kaldor, Mary. 2016. "How peace agreements undermine the rule of law in new war settings." *Global Policy* 7: 146–155.

Kirgis, Frederic L. Jr. 1994. "Editorial Comment; The Degrees of Self-Determination in the United Nations Era." *American Journal of International Law* 88: 304–310.

Klabbers, Jan. 2006. "The Right to be Taken Seriously: Self-determination in International Law." Human Rights Quarterly 28: 186–206.

Knop, Karen. 2008. *Diversity and Self-Determination in International Law*. Cambridge: Cambridge University Press.

Koskenniemi, Martti. 1994. "National Self-Determination Today: Problems of Legal Theory and Practice." *International and Comparative Law Quarterly* 43: 241–269.

Kymlicka, Will. 2007. *Multicultural Odysseys: Navigating the New International Politics of Diversity*. Oxford: Oxford University Press.

Lund, Michael. 2003. *What Kind of Peace is Being Built? Taking Stock of Post-Conflict Peacebuilding and Charting Future Directions*. A discussion paper. Ottawa: International Development Research Centre. http://citeseerx.ist.psu.edu/viewdoc/download?doi=10.1.1.494.1386&rep=rep1&type=pdf.

Mac Ginty, Roger. 2010. "Hybrid Peace: The Interaction between Top-down and Bottom-up Peace." *Security Dialogue* 41: 391–412.

Mac Ginty, Roger. 2011. *International Peacebuilding and Local Resistance: Hybrid Forms of Peace*. Basingstoke: Palgrave Macmillan.

Mac Ginty, Roger and Oliver Richmond. 2015. "The fallacy of constructing hybrid political orders: a reappraisal of the hybrid turn in peacebuilding." *International Peacekeeping* 23: 219–239.

McWhinney, Edward. 2007. *Self-Determination of Peoples and Plural-Ethnic States in Contemporary International Law: Failed States, Nation-Building, and the Alternative, Federal Option*. Dordrecht: Martinus Nijhoff Publishers.

Melandri, Manuela. 2015. "Self-determination and State-building in International Law: The Need for a New Research Approach." *Journal of Conflict and Security Law* 20: 75–100.

Moore, Margaret. 1998. *National Self-Determination and Secession*. Oxford: Oxford University Press.

O'Connell, Mary Ellen. 1992. "Continuing Limits on UN Intervention in Civil War." *Indiana Law Journal* 67: 903–913.

Peace Agreement Access Tool. 1998. Draft Basic Agreement Concerning the Bougainville Reconciliation Government, 24 December 1998, available from https://www.peaceagreements.org/view/370/Draft%20Basic%20 Agreement%20Concerning%20the%20Bougainville%20Reconciliation%20 Government.

Peace Agreement Access Tool. 2002. The third session of peace talks between the Government of Sri Lanka (GOSL) and the Liberation Tigers of Tamil Eelam (LTTE) (Oslo Communique), 5 December 2002, available from https://www.peaceagreements.org/wview/1160/The%20third%20sesson%20 of%20peace%20talks%20between%20the%20Government%20of%20Sri%20 Lanka%20(GOSL)%20and%20the%20Liberation%20Tigers%20of%20 Tamil%20Eelam%20(LTTE)%20(Oslo%20Communique).

Peace Agreement Access Tool. 2003a. Human Rights issues relating to the peace process, 8 February 2003, available from https://www.peaceagreements.org/view/1280/.

Peace Agreement Access Tool. 2003b. Sri Lanka Peace Talks – Agreed Statement on behalf of the Parties, 2 March 2003, available from https://www.peaceagreements.org/masterdocument/1278.

Paris, Roland. 2004. *At War's End: Building Peace After Civil Conflict*. Cambridge: Cambridge University Press.

Pomerance, Michla. 1982. *Self-Determination in Law and Practice. The New Doctrine in the United Nations*. The Hague: Martinus Nijhoff Publishers.

Quinn, David. 2007. "Self-determination Movements and their Outcomes." In *Peace and Conflict 2008*, edited by J. Josheph Hewitt, Jonathan Wilkenfed, and Ted Robert Gurr, 33–38. Boulder: Paradigm Publishers.

Richmond, Oliver. 2009. "Becoming Liberal, Unbecoming Liberalism: Liberal–Local Hybridity via the Everyday as a Response to the Paradoxes of Liberal Peacebuilding." *Journal of Intervention and Statebuilding* 3: 324–344.

Rosas, Allan. 1993. "Internal Self-Determination." In *Modern Law of Self-Determination*, edited by Christian Tomuschat, 225–252. London: Martinus Nijhoff Publishers.

Salmon, Jean. 1993. "Internal Aspects of the Right to Self-Determination: Towards a Democratic Legitimacy Principle." In *Modern Law of Self-Determination*, edited by Christian Tomuschat, 253–282. London: Martinus Nijhoff Publishers.

Sapiano, Jenna, Christine Bell, Kimana Zulueta-Fuelscher, Sumit Bisarya, and Asanga Welikala. 2016. *Constitution-Building in Political Settlement Processes: The Quest for Inclusion*. Stockholm. International Institute for Democracy and Electoral Assistance.

Saul, Matthew. 2011a. "Local Ownership of Post-Conflict Reconstruction in International Law: The Initiation of International Involvement." *Journal of Conflict and Security Law* 16: 165–206.

Saul, Matthew. 2011b. "The Normative Status of Self-Determination in International Law: A Formula for Uncertainty in the Scope and Content of the Right?" *Human Rights Law Review* 11: 609–644.

Security Council Resolution 2282/2016, *Post-conflict peacebuilding*, S/RES/2282 (27 April 2016), available from https://undocs.org/S/RES/2282(2016).

Senaratne, Kalana. 2013. "Internal Self-Determination in International Law: A Critical Third-World Perspective." *Asian Journal of International Law* 3: 305–339.

Sriram, Chandra Lekha. 2008. *Peace as Governance: Power-Sharing, Armed Groups and Contemporary Peace Negotiations*. Basingstoke: Palgrave.

Summers, James. 2007. *Peoples and International Law: How Nationalism and Self-Determination Shape a Contemporary Law of Nations*. Leiden: Martinus Nijhoff Publishers.

Summers, James. 2013. "The Internal and External Aspects of Self-Determination Reconsidered." In *Statehood and Self-Determination: Reconciling Tradition and Modernity in International Law*, edited by Duncan French, 229–249. Cambridge: Cambridge University Press.

Thornberry, Patrick. 1989. "Self-Determination, Minorities, Human Rights: A Review of International Instruments." *International and Comparative Law Quarterly* 38: 867–889.

Thornberry, Patrick. 1993. "The Democratic or Internal Aspect of Self-Determination with Some Remarks on Federalism." In *Modern Law of Self-Determination*, edited by Christian Tomuschat, 101–138. Dordrecht: Martinus Nijhoff Publishers.

Tomuschat, Christian. 1992. "Democratic Pluralism: The Right to Political Opposition." In *The Strength of Diversity: Human Rights and Pluralist Democracy*, edited by Allan Rosas and J Helsegen, 27–48. Dordrecht: Martinus Nijhoff Publishers.

Tomuschat, Christian. 1993. *Modern Law of Self-Determination*. Dordrecht: Martinus Nijhoff Publishers.

Tschirgi, Necla. 2004. *Post-Conflict Peacebuilding Revisited: Achievements, Limitations, Challenges*. A conference paper. New York: WSP International/ IPA Peacebuilding Forum. http://www.operationspaix.net/DATA/DOCUMENT/5766~v~Post-conflict_Peacebuilding_Revisited.pdf.

United Nations, General Assembly and Security Council, *Letter from the Permanent Representatives of Ireland, Mexico and South Africa to the United Nations addressed to the President of the General Assembly and the President of the Security Council*, A/64/868 -S/2010/393(21 July 2010) available from https://undocs.org/en/A/64/868.

United Nations, General Assembly and Security Council, *Letter from Chair of the Advisory Group of Experts on the Review of the Peacebuilding Architecture addressed to the President of the General Assembly and the President of the Security Council*, A/69/968-S/2015/490 (29 June 2015), available from https://undocs.org/en/A/69/968.

United Nations, General Assembly and Security Council, *Letter from the Chair of the Peacebuilding Commission addressed to the President of the General Assembly and the President of the Security Council*, A/72/707–S/2018/43 (18 January 2018), available from https://digitallibrary.un.org/record/1656332/files/A_73_645%26S_2018_1105-EN.pdf.

United Nations, Secretary General, *Letter addressed to the President of the Security Council*, S/2001/988 (23 October 2001), 30 August 2001, available from https://undocs.org/S/2001/988.

United Nations, Statement by the President of the Security Council, *Peacebuilding: towards a comprehensive approach*, S/PRST/2001/5 (20 February 2001).

Valadez, Jorge. 2018. *Deliberative Democracy, Political Legitimacy, and Self-determination in Multi-cultural Societies*. New York: Routledge.

Walter, Christian, Antje von Ungern-Sternberg, and Kavus Abushov. 2014. *Self-Determination and Secession in International Law*. Oxford: Oxford University Press.

Weller, Mark. 2009. "Settling Self-determination Conflicts: Recent Developments." *European Journal of International Law* 20: 111–165.

Werner, Wouter G. 2001. "Self-Determination and Civil War." *Journal of Conflict and Security Law* 6: 171–190.

5

Alternative Approaches to Self-Determination Applied to the Cyprus Conflict

CHARIS VAN DEN BERG AND TOBIAS NOWAK

Whether the United Nations (UN) discourages or encourages self-determination of peoples is a question that is not easy to answer. The position of the UN on self-determination must first be distilled from General Assembly (GA) and Security Council (SC) resolutions and the case law of the International Court of Justice (ICJ). International law on self-determination is criticised for being vague; UN GA Resolution 1514 (XV) (1960), Declaration on the Granting of Independence to Colonial Countries and Peoples, suggests, for example, both by the wording of the title and the preamble, that the intended subject of the resolution would be colonial peoples. Nevertheless, the drafters of the text chose to use general terms ('all peoples have the right to self-determination [...]' and 'Convinced that all peoples have an inalienable right to complete freedom, the exercise of their sovereignty and the integrity of their national territory'). International law on self-determination is also criticised for representing the interests of existing states and thus protecting the status quo in international relations. Furthermore, the answer to the question of whether the UN discourages or encourages self-determination depends on what form of self-determination we are talking about: internal or external self-determination? According to Senese (1989, 19) external self-determination is the idea 'that each people has the right to constitute itself a nation-state or to integrate into, or federate with, an existing state' and internal self-determination refers to 'the right of people to freely choose their own political, economic, and social system'. This does not necessarily require the creation of a new state but can be achieved by receiving autonomy inside existing states.

In this contribution, we argue that the current international legal framework, referred to as the UN paradigm, has a number of shortcomings and is therefore inadequate to answer modern claims involving self-determination, such as the Cyprus conflict. Although internal self-determination is encouraged in limited circumstances, we argue that this approach fundamentally disregards other interests besides state interests and is therefore not able to bring the long-lasting Cyprus conflict to an end. Would alternative approaches to self-determination be more successful?

Inspired by Musgrave's (1997, 148–167) initial distinction between definitions of a people, we explored alternative views on self-determination found in academic literature. These views could be grouped under at least two other schools of thought outside the UN framework (Figure 1). One of these, the balancing approach, suggests that finding a sustainable solution to a conflict should be attempted by respecting and balancing the interests of all groups involved. The outcome of such negotiations is much more open than under the UN approach. The other school, the human rights approach, sees self-determination as a fundamental human right that could hypothetically belong to every ethnic group under very different circumstances. They define a people on the basis of subjective factors of self-consciousness, thereby focusing on ethnic criteria and identifying factors such as a shared history, language, religion and geographical, economic and quantitative factors.

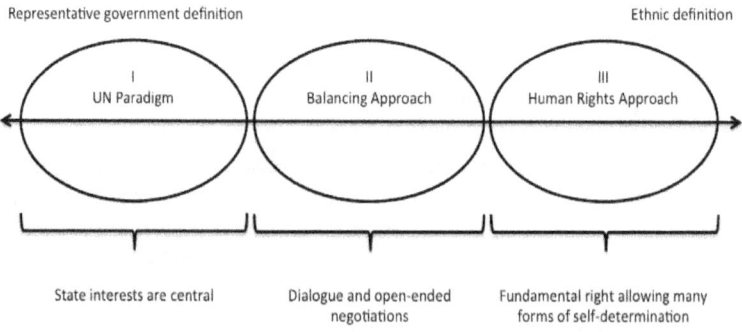

Figure 1: Schools of thought

Each of these schools of thought has consequences for the circumstances in which a successful claim to self-determination can be made, and for the range of peoples that may rightfully do so. To answer the question of whether the UN discourages or encourages self-determination, we will describe how the UN paradigm has fared in the Cyprus conflict. We will then see if either of the other schools offers a better resolution to this conflict than the UN approach does.

The Cyprus Conflict in a Nutshell

Cyprus is an excellent case study of how different visions of self-determination could apply to post-colonial situations. Discussions about the constitutional future of Cyprus were organised after the Second World War. Britain, as the formal administrator of Cyprus, proposed partition of the island, but this idea was refused not only by Greek and Turkish Cypriots themselves, but also by the international community. Greek Cypriots had been advocating their desire for the union of the island with Greece (*enosis*). This in turn led to a Turkish Cypriot call for partition, and thus for Turkish Cypriot independence. The goals of Greek Cypriot irredentism and Turkish Cypriot separation have been totally irreconcilable, yet both have been justified by reference to self-determination (Musgrave 1997, 227).

In 1960, Cyprus became a republic with a constitution based on the political representation of both Cypriot communities. However, political tensions between the two communities remained. Since the outbreak of violence and consequent 1974 division of Cyprus into northern Turkish and southern Greek parts, the UN undertook several efforts to reunite the island under one political administration. Both communities took turns rejecting UN proposals for reconciliation and the reinstitution of a bi-communal (con)federation.[1] See for example UN GA Resolution 37/253 (1983) where the General Assembly deplores the current state of affairs and calls for the continuation of constructive bi-communal deliberate efforts.

In 1983, the Turkish Cypriot Parliament unanimously proclaimed an independent Turkish Republic of Northern Cyprus (TRNC), which was immediately condemned by the Security Council in Resolutions S/RES/541 (1983) and S/RES/550 (1984). The Annan plan was the latest serious effort by the UN to unify Cyprus; it and can be found in report S/2004/437 (2004) of the Secretary-General on his mission of good offices in Cyprus. However, Greek Cyprus rejected this plan in 2004. Later attempts, not only by the UN and by the leaders of the Greek and Turkish Cypriot communities, but also by the European Union, did not amount to much either. Thus, the story of a divided Cyprus continues.

---

[1] www.cyprusun.org provides an overview of GA and SC resolutions concerning the Cyprus conflict (Cyprusun 2012).

UN Paradigm

As the first school of thought, the UN paradigm represents the current and general interpretation of self-determination held by the main organs of the UN. This approach is also supported by contributions in academic literature (Brilmayer 1991, 177–202; Buchanan 2004, 205–208; Gudeleviciute 2005, 48–74; Kirgis 1994, 308). First, we will discuss the general position of the UN with respect to self-determination. Then, we will see how the UN paradigm fared in the context of the Cyprus conflict.

UN Practice

In a sense, the UN has been an advocate of self-determination. Much is owed to the UN for advancing the development of self-determination from a political principle into a legal right, for example by including self-determination as one of the organisation's purposes in the UN Charter.[2] Also in later UN GA resolutions, the right was recognised as a human right and fundamental principle of international law; for example: the Universal Declaration of Human Rights, GA Resolution 217A (III) of 10 December 1948; the Declaration on the Granting of Independence to Colonial Countries, GA Resolution 1514 (XV) of 14 December 1960; the International Covenants on Civil and Political Rights and on Economic, Social and Cultural Rights, GA Resolution 2200 (XXI) of 16 December 1966; the Declaration on Principles of International Law Concerning Friendly Relations and Cooperation Among States in accordance with the Charter of the United Nations, GA Resolution 2625 (XXV) of 24 October 1970; the Declaration on the Occasion of the 50th Anniversary of the UN, GA Resolution 50/6 of 24 October 1995.

The effect of these political acts of the UN has perhaps been clearest with respect to the widespread wave of anti-colonialism that went through the world, culminating in the assertion of the right by many colonial peoples in the period from the 1940s to the 1960s. The ICJ, in landmark cases such as the *Namibia*, *Western Sahara*, and *East Timor* cases, approved of the exercise of self-determination by peoples under colonial or foreign occupation.[3] It has also emphasised that self-determination is an *erga omnes* right, which means

---

[2] See articles 1(2), 55, and Chapters XI, XII, XIII of the Charter, which provide regulations with regard to non-self-governing territories.

[3] See the Namibia case (Legal Consequences for States of the Continued Presence of South Africa in Namibia (South West Africa)) notwithstanding Security Council Resolution 276 (1970), Advisory Opinion, I.C.J. Reports 1971, 16), the Western Sahara case (Western Sahara, Advisory Opinion, I.C.J. Reports 1975, 12) and the East Timor case (East Timor (Portugal v. Australia), Judgment, I.C.J. Reports 1995, 90), all concerning decolonization.

that it can be asserted against any state that infringes this fundamental people's right.[4] Moreover, the ICJ clarified that the right also applies outside the colonial framework, however, within the territorial framework of independent states.[5]

Despite these positive contributions, the UN's practice also suffers from shortcomings and indeterminacies. For example, none of the UN's resolutions contain a formal distinction between internal or external self-determination. Neither does the ICJ, in its extensive set of judgments, make this distinction, nor does it give legal clarification of the circumstances required for a successful claim to external self-determination outside a colonial context. In the *Secession of Quebec*[6] case, the Canadian Supreme Court restated common UN practice, emphasising that 'international law expects that the right to self-determination will be exercised by peoples *within the framework of existing sovereign states* and consistently with the *maintenance of the territorial integrity* of those states [emphasis added], respecting its borders as they have been since independence', in accordance with the principle of *uti possidetis iuris*. The UN has indeed consistently opposed any attempt at the partial or total disruption of the national unity and territorial integrity of a country for reason of maintaining international peace and stability (Shaw 2017, 202). This raises questions of legitimacy and representativeness, especially if these borders were drawn by former occupying parties regardless of historical or ethnic claims to the territory.

While there have been cases in which the ICJ approved of the use of external self-determination, for example in the Palestinian Wall case,[7] this seems to be limited to situations in which human rights are violated as a result of foreign military intervention, aggression, or occupation (including colonialism), or in

---

[4]   See the East Timor case (East Timor (Portugal v. Australia), Judgment, I.C.J. Reports 1995, 90) par. 29, the Barcelona Traction case (Barcelona Traction, Light and Power Company, Limited, Judgment, I.C.J. Reports 1970, 3) par. 33, and the advisory opinion in the Palestinian Wall case (Legal Consequences of the Construction of a Wall in the Occupied Palestinian Territory, Advisory Opinion, I.C.J. Reports 2004, 136) par. 88.

[5]   Burkina Faso v. Republic of Mali case, Judgment, I.C.J. Reports 1986, 554–567, supported by the Canadian Supreme Court in the Secession of Quebec case, Reference re Secession of Quebec, [1998] 2 SCR 217, 1998 CanLII 793 (SCC).

[6]   Secession of Quebec case, Reference re Secession of Quebec, [1998] 2 SCR 217, 1998 CanLII 793 (SCC). Emphasis added. The principle of *uti possidetis iuris* was also mentioned in relation to self-determination in the Burkina Faso v. Mali case (I.C.J. Reports 1986, 554–567), and the Arbitration Commission of the European Conference on Yugoslavia, Opinion no. 2, 92 ILR, 167–168.

[7]   Legal Consequences of the Construction of a Wall in the Occupied Palestinian Territory, Advisory Opinion (I.C.J. Reports 2004, 136).

the most extreme of cases including formal underrepresentation of a minority and serious violations of human rights.[8] Kirgis (1994, 308) formulates this view in the following way:

> If a government is at the high end of the scale of democracy, the only self-determination claims that will be given international credence are those with minimal destabilising effect. If a government is extremely unrepresentative, much more destabilising self-determination claims may well be recognised.

In all other cases, the population of a territory may internally pursue political, economic, social, and cultural development through a participatory democratic process. Moreover, the UN and other international organisations have developed some legal frameworks to protect minorities inside existing states. See for example the Copenhagen Document of what was then called the Conference on Security and Cooperation in Europe (29 June 1990), a charter for regional and minority languages (5 June 1992) and a framework convention for national minorities (February 1995) of the Council of Europe (both entered into force in 1998) and a GA Declaration 47/135 on the rights of persons belonging to certain minorities. Thus, despite promoting the importance of self-determination of *all* peoples in its official documents, the UN seems to adopt a rather conservative approach in practice. State interests generally prevail over the subjective interests of groups in society, so as to prevent the independence and stability of states from being endangered by the challenging of frontiers.

The emphasis on state interests is also reflected in the UN's involvement in peace agreements and negotiations following conflicts concerning claims of self-determination. Although the UN generally takes an optimistic approach by inviting both sides of the conflict into a mediation process, emphasising the importance of non-violent conflict resolution, it nevertheless directs the entire process and does not allow for deviations by either party from the peace agreement. Crucial in this process is the maintenance of political stability and security of state boundaries; see for example S/RES/1410 (2002) on the establishment of a United Nations Mission of Support in East Timor (UNMISET).

Full cooperation of both government and rebellion groups is mandatory and should ideally lead to an inclusive democratic restructuring, thus excluding options that involve territorial changes or extensive political alterations.

---

[8] GA Resolution 72/159 of 19 December 2017, on the universal realization of the right of peoples to self-determination.

Applied to the Cyprus Conflict

How does the UN paradigm fare in the context of the Cyprus conflict? Both key aspects of the UN paradigm – maintaining territorial integrity and interpreting self-determination as an encompassing democratic process – have shaped the UN's policy in the Cyprus conflict. As far back as the late 1950s, when the British proposed partition of the island as the most viable solution to the conflict, the GA asserted their opposition to partition, and therefore external self-determination (Kattan 2015, 22–23). Prior to the colonial declaration (1960), partition was seen as a method or technique of decolonisation and had been applied in a number of cases, for example in the Japanese colony of Korea and French Indochina in 1945 and in British India in 1947 (ibid.). Consecutive resolutions urged the involved parties to respect the full sovereignty, independence, territorial integrity and non-alignment of the Republic of Cyprus and to cease any form of interference with internal affairs.[9] In S/RES/367 (1975) and S/RES/1251 (1999), any attempts at unification with another state or at the partition of the island were expressly condemned. Moreover, the UN SC stated its expectations in S/RES/1251 (1999) about a Cyprus settlement as follows: '[it] must be based on a State of Cyprus with a single sovereignty and international personality and a single citizenship, with its independence and territorial integrity safeguarded, and comprising two politically equal communities [...].' General state interests, meaning keeping the territory intact, have thus prevailed over either community's wishes of partition or unification.

From this perspective it makes sense that the UN SC immediately rejected the unilaterally proclaimed independence of the TRNC in S/RES/541 (1983) and repeated in S/RES/550 (1984). Instead, the Greek-Cypriot government of Cyprus has been regarded as the single representative administration of the entire island until today. In 1993, Greek Cyprus entered into negotiations with the European Union to assess eligibility to European Union membership. In the same year, the European Court of Justice imposed a trade embargo on the TRNC. As tensions on the island remain, the UN SC keeps urging the communities to commit to finding a sustainable solution because the status quo is unacceptable. On this basis, the UN Peacekeeping Force in Cyprus (UNFICYP) is also continued on a yearly basis as confirmed in the latest Resolution S/RES/2453 (2019). Solving the conflict is considered an internal affair that should be solved by both communities on an equal basis and comprising the entire population on the island. In 2001, it was estimated that the ratio of Greek and Turkish Cypriots on the island is nearly 80% to 20% respectively (World Population Review 2019). However, determining the exact

---

[9] See primarily UN GA Resolution 3212 (1974) and UN SC Resolution 365 (1974), and subsequent resolutions.

number of Greek and Turkish Cypriots is not an easy thing and numbers vary. It is unclear who actually counts as a Greek or a Turkish Cypriot. Additionally, both parties tend to exaggerate their own number in this 'war of numbers' (Hatay 2007, 4). Despite numerical differences between the communities, both are referred to by the UN as together being one people. In this way, the UN clearly sees self-determination as an encompassing democratic process.

It is uncertain whether the Cyprus conflict can be solved in the near future as long as the UN paradigm constitutes the standard interpretation. Both communities are confronted with an imposed form of self-determination that depends on their collaboration, while they are scarcely on speaking terms. Maintaining the TRNC does not fit into the picture; the Turkish Cypriots can only receive international recognition for invoking the right to external self-determination if they fall under the exceptional circumstances of non-representation or gross human rights violations. Since UN representatives have made numerous attempts to reconcile both groups, hearing their political expectations and concerns, these exceptional circumstances do not exist. To conclude, the continuous efforts of the UN to bring both communities together into one state structure is an ambitious, but also an unattainable goal which keeps negotiations in a stalemate.

Alternative Approaches

The two alternative views that we composed from academic literature – the balancing and the human rights approach – are both more accommodating towards self-determination than the UN paradigm. The balancing approach discourages the creation of fixed categories of people, and the development of a rigid single legal framework. Rather, flexibility is recommended when it comes to evaluating diverse claims to both internal and external self-determination. The state is no longer considered the most important factor in (inter)national affairs. The human rights approach even takes it a step further by seeing self-determination as a group right potentially belonging to diverse nations or ethnic groups living in the same state. These groups have the right to defend their identities and claims to self-determination must be taken seriously. It therefore takes a sympathetic attitude towards both internal and external forms of self-determination. Both schools will be discussed below.

Balancing Approach

In the balancing approach, flexibility is central. Proponents of this approach argue that neither complete adherence to territorial integrity nor unconditional approval of external self-determination can assure satisfaction on all sides of a dispute (Babbitt 2006; Cassese 1995; Griffiths 2003; Hannum 2006;

Horowitz 1998; McCorquodale 1994). Thus, in each specific situation, a negotiation or reconciliation process involving all parties is recommended. By consent, the parties can choose either to terminate the struggle for self-determination, or to allow for increased internal political rights and autonomy. Claims for external self-determination could even overrule territorial integrity.

Hannum (2006, 76–77), for example, argues that the international community should look for the most appropriate solution to separatist aspirations, in exceptional cases allowing for the creation of a new state. In a similar vein Cassese (1995, 344–362) argues, that the regulation of the right to self-determination is blind to the demands of ethnic groups, and national, religious, cultural, or linguistic minorities, who often find themselves unequipped with rights to improve their situation within existing states. He wants international customary law to develop in such a way as to allow for the free and genuine choice of government in addition to the static model of representative government adopted by the UN. Robert McCorquodale (1994) suggests considering the concept of self-determination as a human right but limited in scope by compelling societal interests, which are protected by the state, but may under no circumstances lead to the oppression of peoples. Horowitz (1998, 181) emphasises that the solution to ethnic territorial claims requires careful balancing to accommodate all interests involved. He suggests that external self-determination would not likely be in everyone's benefit. Martin Griffiths (200, 3) agrees that aspirations to secession are permissible under certain circumstances. Since secession is generally unable to provide the most agreeable solution and will often even appear inadequate, he calls to consider alternatives for secession, such as minority rights. To summarise in the words of Eileen Babbitt (2006, 165):

> As we gain greater understanding of the causes of self-determination conflicts and a better appreciation of the many alternatives that might be put forward to resolve these conflicts, 'negotiating self-determination' may become the norm, rather than the exception.

Balancing Approach Applied to the Cyprus Conflict

Taking a balanced approach to the Cyprus question would first mean not rejecting the aspirations of the Turkish Cypriots to self-determination outright as the UN approach basically does. The goal would be a peaceful solution with which all parties can live, negotiated between the parties. Third parties are helpful if they act as impartial mediators who facilitate meetings between representatives of both sides. Under this approach, an international forum of negotiation would be established. However, contrary to the UN attempts, territorial integrity would not be the ultimate goal. Instead, the outcome is open-ended and could be the status quo, regional autonomy or external self-determination. The revival of the 1960s bi-communal state structure would be a viable option, as would the creation of two states or becoming part of Turkey or Greece. Following the balancing approach, finding the most appropriate solution to the conflict and creating (a) safe and stable political unit(s) on the island in which both peoples are respected and at least sufficiently satisfied, should be an ultimate goal.

Human Rights Approach

The human rights approach comprises diverse critical positions in academic literature against the current standard interpretation of self-determination (Koskenniemi 1994; Margalit and Raz 1990; Pavković 2003; Philpott 1995). Instead of seeing self-determination as a democratic process that involves an entire population, as the UN does, the human rights approach focuses on ethnicity and nationality as the binding elements in societies. According to Daniel Philpott (1995, 353), self-determination is equally essential to a people as is freedom to an individual. For a group, it is the most important instrument in the process of social growth towards their specific social (or economic, legal, political) ideals. As self-determination is a human right that belongs to every (ethnic) group, this approach is also very lenient on the admissibility of many forms of self-determination to assert this right in practice. For instance, secession from an existing state could be an option under certain circumstances. However, a necessary restriction of the *prima facie* right to self-determination is sought by each author from a different perspective; all groups of peoples do possess a fundamental right to self-determination, but it would not be preferential if each group were in a position to assert this right.

Margalit and Raz (1990, 439–461), for example, find the necessary restriction in the applicability of ethnic and social factors. Self-determination would qualify as an instrument for social groups to retain or preserve their identity and to protect themselves against (cultural) oppression by other cultures. It is a right that may belong to a group that forms a majority in a certain territory and shares the same political ideal (Margalit and Raz 1990, 457):

> That importance makes it reasonable to let the encompassing group that forms a substantial majority in a territory have the right to determine whether that territory shall form an independent state in order to protect the culture and self-respect of the group, provided that the new state is likely to respect the fundamental interests of its inhabitants, and provided that

measures are adopted to prevent its creation from gravely damaging the just interests of other countries.

In this view, the possibility of changes in a state's territory is made subordinate to subjective group interests, provided that the group acts responsibly.

Human Rights Approach Applied to the Cyprus Conflict

In general, the human rights approach seems most promising to minorities within states that wish to pursue their political aspirations. The notion of cultural distinctness of a group, which is central to the human rights approach, implies that the Greek-Cypriot and the Turkish-Cypriot communities should not be considered one people. Both communities differ on aspects of ethnicity, language, culture, and history. They have a different set of social ideals and have different ideas about how politics or law can accommodate their group identity. From this perspective, the UN's solution, namely, forcing these distinct groups to commit to the same political ideas under one constitution, appears unrealistic. Both the Greek-Cypriot and the Turkish-Cypriot communities may qualify as encompassing groups as they constitute a numerical majority on their respective territories on the island. If they acted responsibly and represented the political will of the majority, then external self-determination could be a vital method in the preservation of each group's identity and cultural distinctness. There would be more respect and understanding from the international community for the Turkish-Cypriot feeling of cultural distinctness and, accordingly, their declaration of the TRNC. Since the human rights approach adopts a less fixed notion of the execution of the right to self-determination, diverse claims of self-determination can be made – including secession. In this respect, the division of the island along the lines of the two communities could be a viable solution to the conflict.

Conclusions

So, does the UN discourage or encourage self-determination of peoples? Under the exceptional circumstances of the decolonisation process, the UN supported self-determination of colonial peoples. Nowadays, the UN has a clear preference for internal over external self-determination. Especially in the last decade of the twentieth century, efforts have been made – not only by the UN – to ensure that minorities should enjoy the greatest amount of self-determination as is possible in their particular situation. Thus, alternative solutions to secession have been created. This way, the state would remain intact, but a political process of devolution and the granting of partial autonomy would meet minorities in their aspirations to self-determination. When it comes to external self-determination, however, the UN is more reluctant to give in. Claims to secession take second place behind the territorial integrity of a state. For the Cyprus conflict this means that a single state including both communities is the only acceptable solution.

The alternative approaches suggested in the academic literature are much less state-centric and more favourable towards external self-determination. When compared to these approaches, the UN approach looks like a strong opponent of external self-determination. Although looking at the Cyprus conflict through the eyes of the alternative approaches revealed different solutions that cannot be imagined under the UN paradigm, they are far from providing a realistic solution to the conflict. For any of the alternative approaches to have a real impact on international politics, a paradigm shift supported by the international community away from the UN paradigm towards one of the alternative approaches has to occur.

References

Babbitt, Eileen F. 2006. "Negotiating Self-Determination. Is it a Viable Alternative to Violence?". In *Negotiating Self-Determination*, edited by Hurst Hannum and Eileen F. Babbitt, 159–165. Lanham: Lexington Books.

Brilmayer, Lea. 1991. "Secession and Self-Determination: a Territorial Interpretation." *Yale Journal of International Law* 16: 177–202.

Buchanan, Allen. 2004. *Justice, Legitimacy, and Self-Determination. Moral Foundations for International Law*. Oxford: Oxford University Press.

Cassese, Antonio. 1995. *Self-Determination of Peoples: A Legal Reappraisal*. Cambridge: Cambridge University Press.

Conference on Security and Cooperation in Europe. 1990. *Document of the Copenhagen meeting of the Conference on the Human Dimension of the CSCE*, available from https://www.osce.org/odihr/elections/14304?download=true.

Council of Europe. 1992. *European Charter for Regional and Minority Languages*. European Treaty Series-No. 148, available from https://www.coe.int/en/web/conventions/full-list/-/conventions/rms/0900001680695175.

Council of Europe. 1995. *Framework Convention for the Protection of National Minorities and Explanatory Report*. H (95) 10, available from https://rm.coe.int/CoERMPublicCommonSearchServices DisplayDCTMContent?documentId=09000016800c10cf.

Cyprusun. 2012. "UN Documents on Cyprus - Reports". Accessed June 31, 2019. http://www.cyprusun.org/?cat=52.

General Assembly Resolution 217A (III), *International bill of human rights - universal declaration of human rights*, A/RES/217(III) (10 December 1948), available from https://undocs.org/en/A/RES/217(III).

General Assembly Resolution 1514 (XV), *Declaration of the granting of independence to colonial countries and peoples*, A/RES/1514(XV) (14 December 1960), available from https://undocs.org/en/A/RES/1514(XV).

General Assembly Resolution 2200 (XXI), *International covenants on civil and political rights and on economic, social and cultural rights*, A/RES/2200 (XXI) (16 December 1966), available from https://undocs.org/en/A/RES/2200(XXI).

General Assembly Resolution 2625 (XXV), *Declaration on principles of international law concerning friendly relations and cooperation among states in accordance with the Charter of the United Nations*, A/RES/2625(XXV) (24 October 1970), available from https://undocs.org/en/A/RES/2625(XXV).

General Assembly Resolution 3212 (XXIX), *Questions of Cyprus*, A/RES/3212 (XXIX) (1 November 1974), available from https://undocs.org/en/A/RES/3212(XXIX).

General Assembly Resolution 37/253, *Question of Cyprus*, A/RES/37/253 (13 May 1983), available from https://undocs.org/en/A/RES/37/253.

General Assembly Resolution 47/135, *Declaration on the rights of persons belonging to national or ethnic, religious and linguistic minorities*, A/RES/47/135 (18 December 1992), available from https://www.un.org/documents/ga/res/47/a47r135.htm.

General Assembly Resolution 50/6, *Declaration on the occasion of the fiftieth anniversary of the United Nations*, A/RES/50/6 (24 October 1995), available from https://undocs.org/en/A/RES/50/6.

General Assembly Resolution 72/159, *Universal realization of the right of peoples to self-determination*, A/RES/72/159 (19 December 2017), available from https://undocs.org/en/A/RES/72/159.

Gudeleviciute, Vita. 2005. "Does the principle of self-determination prevail over the principle of territorial integrity?" *International Journal of Baltic Law* 2 (2): 48–74.

Griffiths, Martin. 2003. "Self-Determination, International Society and World Order." *Macquarie Law Journal* 3: 29–49.

Hannum, Hurst. 2006. "Self-Determination in the Twenty-First Century." In *Negotiating Self-Determination*, edited by Hurst Hannum and Eileen F. Babbitt, 61–80. Lanham: Lexington Books.

Hatay, Mete. 2007. "Is the Turkish Cypriot Population Shrinking? An Overview of the Ethno-Demography of Cyprus in the Light of the Preliminary Results of the 2006 Turkish-Cypriot Census." International Peace Research Institute: Oslo. https://www.prio.org/Global/upload/Cyprus/Publications/Is%20the%20Turkish%20Cypriot%20Population%20Shrinking.pdf.

Horowitz, Donald L. 1998. "Self-Determination: Politics, Philosophy, and Law." In *National Self-Determination and Secession*, edited by Margaret Moore, 181–215. Oxford: Oxford University Press.

Kattan, Victor. 2015. "Self-Determination during the Cold War: UN General Assembly Resolution 1514 (1960), the Prohibition of Partition, and the Establishment of the British Indian Ocean Territory (1965)." *Max Planck Yearbook of United Nations Law* 19: 419–468.

Kirgis, Frederic L. Jr. 1994. "The Degrees of Self-Determination in the United Nations Era." *The American Journal of International Law* 88 (2): 304–310.

Koskenniemi, Martti. 1994. "National Self-Determination Today: Problems of Legal Theory and Practice." *International and Comparative Law Quarterly* 43 (2): 241–269.

Margalit, Avishai and Joseph Raz. 1990. "National Self-Determination." *The Journal of Philosophy* 87 (9): 439–461.

McCorquodale, Robert. 1994. "Self-Determination: A Human Rights Approach." *The International and Comparative Law Quarterly* 43 (4): 857–885.

Musgrave, Thomas. D. 1997. *Self-Determination and National Minorities*. Oxford: Oxford University Press.

Pavković, Aleksandar. 2003. "Secession, Majority Rule and Equal Rights: A Few Questions." *Macquarie Law Journal* 3: 73–94.

Philpott, Daniel. 1995. "In Defence of Self-Determination." *Ethics* 105 (2): 352–385.

Security Council report 2004/437, *Report of the Secretary-General on his mission of good offices in Cyprus*, S/2004/437 (28 May 2004), available from https://documents-dds-ny.un.org/doc/UNDOC/GEN/N04/361/53/PDF/N0436153.pdf?.

Security Council Resolution 276, *The situation in Namibia*, S/RES/276 (30 January 1070), available from http://unscr.com/en/Resolutions/doc/276.

Security Council Resolution 365, *Cyprus*, S/RES/365 (13 December1974).

Security Council Resolution 367, *Cyprus*, S/RES/367 (12 March 1975) available from https://undocs.org/S/RES/367.

Security Council Resolution 541, *Cyprus*, S/RES/541 (18 November 1983).

Security Council Resolution 550, *Cyprus*, S/RES/550 (11 May 1984), available from https://undocs.org/S/RES/550 (1984).

Security Council Resolution 1251, *Cyprus*, S/RES/1251 (29 June 1999) available from https://undocs.org/S/RES/1251 (1999).

Security Council Resolution 1410, *East Timor*, S/RES/1410 (17 May 2002), available from https://undocs.org/S/RES/1410 (2002).

Security Council Resolution 2453, *The situation in Cyprus*, S/RES/2453 (30 January 2019), available from https://undocs.org/S/RES/2453 (2019).

Senese, Salvatore. 1989. "External and Internal Self-Determination." *Social Justice* 16 (1): 19–25.

Shaw, Malcolm N. 2017. *International Law*. 8th edition. Cambridge: University Press.

United Nations. 1945. *Charter of the United Nations and Statute of the International Court of Justice* (adopted 26 June 1945, entered into force 23 March 1945) 59 Stat. 1031, available from https://www.un.org/en/sections/un-charter/introductory-note/index.html.

World Population Review. 2019. "Population Cyprus". Accessed June 32, 2019. http://worldpopulationreview.com/countries/cyprus-population/.

6

The United Nations, Self-Determination, State Failure and Secession

ED BROWN

As this chapter will find, the United Nations (UN) has made several declarations concerning self-determination; the stance of the UN on self-determination can appear somewhat contradictory at times, expressing support at various times for both self-determination and for territorial integrity (the inviolability of borders). Despite such ambiguity, the position of the UN on secession and any subsequent recognition is particularly important since accession to the UN is considered by the international community as tantamount to near-universal recognition. To become a member, a state must be recognised by at least two-thirds[1] of existing members after gaining approval of the UN Security Council, which implies that it has the recognition of the major world powers, i.e. the permanent members (P-5) (UN 2019).

The chapter investigates whether the UN stance on self-determination and secession, makes it a friend or foe to self-determination in the context of failed states. The purpose of this chapter is to analyse the balance of legitimacy between the secessionists and the parent state, given the argument that a failed state has a deficit of legitimacy, and to analyse the UN stance from both an ethical and a practical perspective in light of this. Firstly, what the stance of the UN on self-determination might be is considered, and then the concept of state failure is introduced, while noting how secession from a failed state fits within the UN stance. Finally, two actual cases of secession from failed states will be examined; the secession of South Sudan,

---

[1] Whilst accession to the UN does not necessarily mean a state has achieved universal recognition, most members who vote in the UN General Assembly are generally recognised to be states (Aust 2005, 18).

which became a UN member, and the *de facto* secession of Somaliland, which so far has not acceded to the UN. This will allow the chapter to ascertain whether the UN stance makes it a friend or foe to self-determination in this particular context.

The main conceptual framework comes from the situation when a people are not having their security protected by their parent state, which then fits into what is known as the 'Remedial Right to Secede' (RRS) (Buchanan 1997, 35). This is loosely based on John Locke's 'Right to Revolution' (ibid.); the idea that if a group has their rights abused by the sovereign, then they have a right to look for a new sovereign. Whilst this could be achieved through democracy or revolution for individuals, writers such as Buchanan (1997, 37) have argued that this could include creating a new sovereign by establishing a new state. Essentially, it means that if the government is not upholding its side of the social contract, i.e. providing security to its citizens, including the individuals within a secessionist entity, then it forfeits a degree of legitimacy. If a secessionist state is able to better provide said security, then the legitimacy of their claim to statehood may increase and a stronger case for recognition can be made.

The idea of the RRS can be seen, in this way, to complement the Responsibility to Protect (R2P), the idea that sovereignty is dependent on responsibility, in so much that sovereignty and legitimacy are based upon the responsibility of the state in question (Brown 2018, 88–89). This in turn shows that with R2P being brought to the fore in the UN, self-determination through the RRS can be tacitly supported to admit new members to the UN, as the case studies in this chapter both infer. The RRS is compatible with the idea that sovereignty is based on responsibility, and thus if R2P is ostensibly supported within the UN, so too can remedial secession be. This chapter further argues that this right can apply when a parent state is *unable* to uphold the security of all of its citizens, thus *passively* undermining the basic rights of its citizens (including those in a secessionist entity) and where a secessionist entity is better able to do so, thus gaining the balance of legitimacy. Whether states take this into account when considering recognition of new states can determine whether a state accedes to the UN. Therefore, it is important to consider how UN principles on self-determination apply to secession from failed states and how UN principles on self-determination can be interpreted in such a context and particularly, if and how these principles are followed by the international community in this context.

This chapter analyses the ambiguities in the UN stance towards secession in the context of failed states. It assesses whether the UN is a friend or foe in these cases by looking at where exceptions could be or, in the case of the first case study, have been made to what is ostensibly an anti-secessionist stance and the reasoning behind these exceptions. Also, in the second case study, it examines where the conditions for these exceptions are arguably present, but not made. The chapter concludes by arguing that whilst this stance is inconsistent and possibly in need of reform, by keeping its stance ambiguous the UN can act pragmatically in cases where secession from a failed state may ease a conflict without setting a precedent that may undermine the international system of states. This shows that, in this context, the UN can show itself to be a friend to self-determination, but only if expedient to do so (i.e. it helps to resolve a conflict) and does not go against the interests of major powers.

Definitions

Self-Determination

Whilst this chapter deals primarily with self-determination through secession, the UN describes the different modes of self-determination that can occur as 'The establishment of a sovereign and independent state, the free association or integration with an independent state or the emergence into any other political status freely determined by a people constitute modes of implementing the right of self-determination by that people' (A/RES/2625(XXV)). The ambiguity arising from the multiple definitions of self-determination can be dangerous, since it may lead to impasse and conflict where a group believes that they have a right to full independence whilst other actors, such as the parent state, may believe that they have the right to a degree of autonomy or representation in exercising their right to self-determination, but not have a right of secession. For example, James Anaya (1996, 333) differentiates between different modes of self-determination, looking at two specific models:

1. 'Constitutive self-determination', whereby a people decide on their future status, opting for or rejecting secession, as has been illustrated in independence referenda such as those in recent times of Scotland, South Sudan and Montenegro (the latter two resulting in independence, the former not); and

2. 'Ongoing self-determination', whereby a group exercises a degree of political control over its own people and/or territory, although not necessarily through full independence as the constituent countries of the United Kingdom currently do (2019),[2] or federal subjects of federal countries such as Russia or the United States of America.

---

[2] Scotland can be seen as an example of both forms of self-determination, since it held a referendum on independence as well as holding a degree of autonomy through the Scottish Parliament.

The extent of self-determination and self-government is difficult to quantify given the number of forms such an arrangement could take. With this in mind, Buchanan (2004, 333) notes that '[I]t is extraordinarily unhelpful to talk about "the" right to self-determination (or autonomy). Yet existing international law contains dangerously ambiguous references to "the right of self-determination of peoples"'. The many different forms which self-determination has taken throughout the world in the past suggests there is a degree of method to the madness when it comes to the ambiguous nature of states' approaches on the matter. Having multiple definitions of self-determination allows the potential recognising actors to adopt a degree of pragmatism in their approach, as it allows all options to be explored before resorting to recognising the independence of a secessionist state. It also allows for each case to be approached on an individual basis. This is beneficial to the UN approach since, whilst cases of secession may bear similarities to each other, no two cases will be exactly the same. Each instance will have a unique set of needs and will have to be approached in a unique manner. Keeping the law ambiguous allows the UN to tailor its approach to the specific situation, which more specific and rigid laws on the issue would prevent.

This chapter looks at the use of the definition of constitutive self-determination as self- determination exercised through secession. However, it acknowledges that the definition of self-determination is open to interpretation and forms of ongoing self-determination may be favoured if in the interest of states within the international community.

Secession

Secession is the act of defying the rule of the parent state, not through revolution or otherwise trying to change the government of the state, but to exclude the jurisdiction of the parent state from the claimed territory of the secessionists (Buchanan 1991, 10). Whether or not a secessionist entity is indeed a state depends on the theory of state one is using. The *declaratory theory of secession* echoes the Declaration of the Montevideo Convention on the Rights and Duties of States, in that a state exists if it possesses a permanent population, a defined territory, a government and the capacity to enter into relations with other states; if a state fulfils these criteria then it exists regardless of recognition (Eckert 2002, 21). On the other hand, the *constitutive theory of secession* puts more emphasis on *recognition* of statehood rather than statehood alone (Eckert 2002, 24). Whilst the declaratory theory asserts that the existence of a state is independent of recognition, the constitutive theory stresses that for a state to exist it must receive formal recognition specifically, as well as possess the capacity to enter into relations with other states, which many unrecognised states have the ability to do (ibid.).

It would appear that it is the constitutive theory of state that is important for accession to the UN (how this chapter would define a successful secession), since an entity must be recognised as a state by at least two-thirds of the General Assembly (GA) and by the Security Council (SC) to become a member. The implications of this for this chapter are that UN admission is dependent on recognition from states within the international community, thus prospective member-states are at the mercy of how UN declarations based on the right to self-determination are interpreted by the current member-states, who may interpret and apply them differently based on self-interest and/or pragmatism.

State Failure

The concept and definition of a so-called failed state is varied and contested. This is reflected in the sheer number of different indices, such as the *Fund For Peace/Foreign Policy* 'Fragile States Index', the Global Peace Index, George Mason University's State Fragility Index, World Bank Group's Harmonized List of Fragile Situations and the Center for Systemic Peace's Polity project (Brown 2018, 132–139). These indices use a range of factors. However, for the sake of conciseness, we will use a definition based on the works of Max Weber, who stated that a successful state is one that has the monopoly on the legitimate use of force and thus a failed state is one which either loses the monopoly or the legitimacy (Weber 1919).[3] This phenomenon can be seen in most of the states that rank highly in the aforementioned indices (Brown 2018, 122 and 138). States can lose the *legitimacy* of their use of force by using it in an illegitimate manner, for example by persecuting a group. A state can lose the *monopoly* on the use of force by losing control over its territory, for example if non-governmental armed groups become active within their recognised borders and cannot be controlled by governmental forces. At times, an oppressed group will fight back, and civil war will ensue, as happened in Sudan, in which case the parent state can be said to have lost both the monopoly *and* the legitimacy of the use of force.

Security

For the purposes of this chapter the definition of security is taken from the *Fragile States Index* by Fund For Peace (2019, 34):

---

[3] It must be noted that Weber was a sociologist, however, in this context he was discussing the role of force in statehood, an issue which crosses the disciplines of sociology and politics.

> The Security Apparatus indicator considers the security threats to a state, such as bombings, attacks and battle-related deaths, rebel movements, mutinies, coups, or terrorism. The Security Apparatus indicator also takes into account serious criminal factors, such as organised crime and homicides, and perceived trust of citizens in domestic security.

When this chapter refers to the ability of a state to uphold citizens' security, it is referring to its ability to mitigate the threats to security outlined above, and, as it says, the confidence a state's citizens have in their ability to do this. A state can fail to mitigate security threats and/or maintain the confidence of its citizens either passively, by lacking the means to mitigate threats, or actively, by undermining security through abuses of power such as oppression and persecution.

Conceptualisation

The UN, Self-Determination and Secession

The UN Charter (1945) expresses the position that peoples have the right to self-determination in Article 1 of Chapter 1, however in Article 2 it also makes clear that the integrity of states is vital. According to the Declaration on the Granting of Independence to Colonial Countries and Peoples this can be applied to the promotion of secession within a third-party country as 'any attempt aimed at the *partial or total disruption of the national unity* and the territorial integrity of a country is incompatible with the purposes and principles of the Charter of the United Nations' (A/RES/1514(XV) [emphasis added]). Whilst this declaration concerns decolonisation rather than secession and aims to differentiate between the two by advocating decolonisation but not secession, one of the arguments of this chapter is that secession often occurs when a people are oppressed by a parent state that does not represent them. This is, in principle, similar to a colony working towards independence. Indeed, in the context of South Sudan, Sharkey (2008, 6) referred to the rule over the South by the oppressive, non-representative North as 'cultural colonialism'.

A rationale for this ambiguity is implied by the UN in so much that the territorial integrity of sovereign states is an international norm. This is because allowing a general right to self-determination through secession could result in a proliferation of states that would undermine the international system of states. As Buchanan (1991, 102) points out, 'If large groups are allowed to secede, why not small groups…why not individuals?'. Such an argument paints secession as something of a Pandora's box, that once opened would undermine global order, security and stability as we know it. This concern has been shared by other International Relations scholars such as Pavkovic and Radan (2007, 129) who talk of 'recursive secession', that is, secession from a state that has itself seceded, and 'sequential secession', a further secession from the same parent state. An example of the former would be the secession of South Ossetia and Abkhazia from Georgia, and an example of the latter would be the different states that seceded from Yugoslavia.

With this in mind it would seem logical for the UN to favour the concept of ongoing self-determination rather than constitutive self-determination where it can. However, as Buchanan (1991, 102) rightly goes on to say, this argument is based on the premise that the right to secede is an unlimited right to secede, in other words an inherent right to secession held by all peoples. In reality however, there are limits to such sovereignty and territorial integrity.

This is observable in the UN Declaration on Principles of International Law Concerning Friendly Relations and Co-operation among States in accordance with the Charter of the United Nations (A/RES/2625(XXV)), which, amongst many principles surrounding the promotion between states of cooperation and friendly relations, includes 'the principle of equal rights and self-determination of peoples.' Pavkovic and Radan (2007, 235) observe in this principle that 'A state's right to territorial integrity prevails over the right of any of its peoples to self-determination, *provided that state conducts itself in accordance with the principles of equal rights and self-determination of peoples*' [emphasis added].

This is most observable in the Declaration's section on *the principle of equal rights and self-determination of peoples*, where it is stated that territorial integrity is only protected if the state in question has 'a government representing the whole people belonging to the territory without distinction as to race, creed or colour'. This can be interpreted as the state having a responsibility to represent minorities within its territory (Pavkovic and Radan 2007, 235). It also implies that should a state fail to uphold the rights of these minorities or, worse, persecute the peoples involved, then secession could be justified, and the secessionist entity recognised. To this extent territorial integrity appears conditional upon the sovereign's ability to uphold it responsibly, since a state cannot expect to have its sovereignty and therefore its borders respected if a) it abuses its sovereignty to perpetrate human rights breaches, and b) it appears unable to uphold said sovereignty by failing to provide security for its citizens. This would suggest that territorial integrity is conditional upon the state upholding its duties towards its citizens, including minorities and thus proving itself responsible for their rights. This fits in with the idea of remedial secession as previously discussed.

A/RES/545(VI) goes even further, reaffirming the right to self-determination by noting that 'the violation of this right [to self-determination] has resulted in bloodshed and war in the past and is considered a threat to peace'. Whilst this can apply to violation of self-determination through colonisation, it is also true, as will be seen in the case study on South Sudan, that bloodshed and war can also result through a denial of ongoing self-determination of a group within a state's borders. Thus, the right to self-determination is reaffirmed in this instance.

The argument of this chapter that secession from failed states is distinct from general secession is based on the idea that sovereignty is conditional. This idea is supported by the evolving consensus on R2P within the UN; that is, a state has the responsibility to protect the security of its population, in particular to protect it from 'genocide, war crimes, ethnic cleansing and crimes against humanity' (UN Office on Genocide Prevention and the Responsibility to Protect 2019). The third pillar of the R2P doctrine states that 'If a State is manifestly failing to protect its populations, the international community must be prepared to take collective action to protect populations, in accordance with the Charter of the United Nations' (UN 2012). A report from the UN Secretary-General on R2P noted that 'Responsible sovereignty is based on the politics of inclusion, not exclusion' (A/63/677). This implies that a state's sovereignty and territorial integrity are dependent upon upholding them. Thus, there can be a legitimate claim for recognition of a prospective secessionist state based around such a minority or group if the parent state is not upholding the rights of these people.[4] The idea that the breaching R2P principles can undermine a state's sovereignty has in general been used as a rationale for humanitarian intervention rather than secession. However, Janik (2013, 57–58) hypothesised that humanitarian intervention may lead to intervention in support of secessionist groups if said secessionists are facing persecution, invoking the remedial right to secede and suggesting that such support could in fact encourage secessionist movements. The idea that the Responsibility to Protect could encourage secessionist movements is supported by Kuperman (2009, 22), who suggests that '[G]enocide and ethnic cleansing often represent state retaliation against a sub-state group for rebellion, or armed secession'. Should this be the case then states may intervene on the side of secessionists under the responsibility to protect, thus potentially increasing support for the secession that could conceivably lead to

---

[4] It must be noted that it is not always mistreated minorities that want to secede; however, this chapter is exploring the idea that minorities within a failed state which is unwilling and/or unable to uphold minority rights, and in some cases have been actively persecuted, have a case for UN membership based on the remedial right to secede.

recognition, as in the case of Bosnia and Herzegovina, for example (Janik 2013, 57–60).

The Issue of State Failure

The issue with states that either lose the monopoly or the legitimacy of the force as outlined in the Weberian definition of state failure, is that they will generally either be unable or unwilling to provide basic rights such as security to their citizens. This arguably means that they are unwilling or unable to adhere to the principles of the norm that is the R2P since the state would be 'manifestly failing to protect its populations' as supported in the UN resolution following the 2005 World Summit Outcome (A/RES/60/1). Additionally, such a state would be unlikely to be willing or able to uphold minority rights and thus support the self-determination of peoples within its borders as extolled by the UN Declaration on Friendly Relations (Pavkovic and Radan 2007, 235). This would be the case for a failed state almost by definition, since if it were unable to maintain the monopoly of legitimate force it would be unable to uphold such rights. If the use of force was illegitimate, i.e. being used for the purposes of oppression, then the government in question would not be representative of such a minority. The above definition of state failure refers to the state's ability to provide basic rights and security to all its citizens. However, it is of particular interest and importance if there is a distinct minority within that state who are being directly oppressed by the parent state, are otherwise disproportionately disadvantaged by the failings of the state. It is also of particular interest if said minority has managed to establish order and effective governance within their own region where disorder and lack of legitimate government control is spread throughout the rest of the parent state.

Both phenomena arguably fit in with the aforementioned remedial right to secede, as in both cases the parent state is not upholding its side of the social contract. The first of these phenomena is seen in the first case study of this chapter, South Sudan, whose security and basic human rights had been actively undermined by persecution from the parent state of Sudan. The second of these phenomena is seen in the second case study of the chapter, Somaliland, which has managed to establish a stable government despite the lack of control of the government of parent state Somalia over its claimed territory. The case of South Sudan, as will be seen, would suggest a shifting paradigm within the UN towards further emphasis on the conditions being put on sovereignty such as those observed in 'the principle of equal rights and self-determination of peoples' of the UN Declaration on Friendly Relations and as endorsed by R2P. This in turn has the potential to create a more conducive environment for self-determination within the UN for peoples whose parent states lack legitimacy. This means that the predilection in the UN for supporting territorial integrity over self-determination via secession, as observed earlier in the chapter, could be diminished in cases where the sovereignty of the parent state is compromised by state failure i.e. losing the legitimacy of its use of force, or losing its monopoly on the legitimate use of force. This is shown through the fact that whilst Somaliland has yet to become a UN member, in both cases the ability of the state to provide basic human rights and security is greatly compromised and the remedial right to secede can be invoked.

Additionally, it has been claimed by former UN Secretary-General Boutros Boutros-Ghali in reference to Somalia that the inability of a state to govern erodes its sovereignty (UN 1996, 87):

> A state that loses its government...loses its place as a member of the international community...The charter of the United Nations provides for the admission to the international community of a country which gains the attributes of sovereignty...It does not, however, provide for any mechanisms through which the international community can respond when a sovereign State loses one of the attributes of statehood.

It is important to note, however, that this lack of sovereignty does not preclude the existence of the state in question, whilst the sovereignty of a failed state may be compromised in practice, it is still a state in international law and a member of the UN. For example, Somalia, a state whose government has had extremely limited control over its territory for decades, is still a member of the UN. States that lack the ability to govern are still recognised because, as Potter (2004, 11–12) writes, there are two practical aspects of sovereignty that exist side by side: external and internal sovereignty; external sovereignty refers to the recognition of a state by other states, while internal sovereignty refers to the state upholding its responsibilities to its citizens. As this chapter argues, this loss of internal sovereignty among other factors can be used to justify the admission of a secessionist state to the UN if it is governing its territory more effectively than the parent state as a case for remedial secession exists. However, this does not preclude the existence of the parent state, the remainder of the parent state can remain recognised despite its compromised sovereignty leading to secession.

The lack of legitimacy and sovereignty of the parent state, along with the perceived rising legitimacy of the secessionist state has been used to justify the recognition of secession in the past. The example of this phenomena that this chapter will look at is the secession of South Sudan. It must once again be stressed that the UN did not have a direct role in the recognition of these secessions, it is not the UN itself that 'recognises' states, but the member states that make up the UN. However, it is important to analyse the way in which these secessions were handled by the states involved in order to show how secession from failed states has been handled by states within the wider international community, how South Sudan came to accede to the UN and how its recognition fits in with the UN principles on territorial integrity and self-determination. Likewise, the as-yet unrecognised secession of Somaliland will be examined in order to assess why it has not gained membership despite the case for it. This will in turn enable the chapter to understand more about the attitude of the UN towards secession from failed states, as well as a consideration of the suitability of this approach in moral and practical terms.

Case Study: South Sudan

Fitting in with the idea of secession based on R2P and RRS, South Sudan acceded to the UN in 2011. Its split from Sudan had been based upon both resolution of the civil war that had been continuing intermittently for decades and the oppression and subjugation of the South by the Khartoum government prior to, and during, said civil war which had demonstrated Khartoum's inability to protect its citizens, which, as argued in this chapter, can be grounds for remedial secession (Brown 2018, 230). Importantly, many in the South saw this subjugation as 'cultural colonialism' on the part of the Khartoum government (Sharkey 2008, 36). This was due to the 'Arabisation' movement, whereby the Christian, English-speaking identity of the South was denied, indeed, the Southern Federal Party's request that English and Christianity be included as an official language and religion alongside Arabic and Islam, were met with criminal prosecutions (Sharkey 2008, 34–36). This can be seen to contravene UN General Assembly Resolution 2625(XXV), which as seen earlier stipulates that a government must represent all its citizens regardless of race or religion. The ensuing Civil War also invokes UN General Assembly Resolution 545(VI), which reaffirms the right to self-determination when its violation leads to war and bloodshed.

This indicates that, whilst UNGA resolutions are not obligatory for states, it does show that the UN is, in principle at least, something of a friend to self-determination in this context, since in this instance violating this UN principle indeed initiated a process whereby a remedial secession achieved UN membership, as South Sudan did.

Here we see two potential motives for the recognition of a secessionist state, pragmatic conflict resolution, and a moral case based on the oppression of a people. Indeed, both the need to end the civil war, and the past injustices towards the South were noted in the Comprehensive Peace Agreement (CPA) (UNMIS 2005).

It is important to note that the pragmatic course of action can also be the moral one, whilst achieving peace and achieving justice can be seen to be different things, in this case the one could arguably have come with the other.[5] The referendum on the independence of South Sudan was won overwhelmingly, 99.57% voting in favour of South Sudanese secession (BBC 2011). This referendum was part of the CPA under the auspices of the Intergovernmental Authority on Development (IGAD), with which the UN was heavily involved, to end the civil war, in the course of the negotiations such a concession had seemed necessary. UN involvement included providing 'technical and logistical assistance to the CPA parties' referendum preparations through support from its peacekeeping missions on the ground in Sudan, as well as the good offices function provided by the Secretary-General's panel aimed at ensuring the impartiality, independence and effectiveness of the process, and by the UN Integrated Referenda and Electoral Division (UNIRED)' (UNMIS, 2005).

This necessity can be seen as being due to a lack of trust in Khartoum by the South. This mistrust is illustrated by the failure of previous peace agreements such as the Addis Ababa Agreement (UN Peacemaker 1972; Brown 2018, 207). This agreement had granted a degree of autonomy short of independence to the South but failed after President Ga'afar Nimeiri enforced Sharia Law over the predominantly Christian South, again plunging the country into civil war (Woodward 1990, 156–157; Brown 2018, 233–234 and 254–255). This also illustrates the tip in the balance of legitimacy towards the secessionists, since a decline in legitimacy of the parent state due to rights abuses was met with a perceived rise in legitimacy of the secessionist state, as illustrated by the referendum.[6]

It is worth mentioning at this point that the religious aspect of the conflict may have influenced the recognition of South Sudan in that the independence movement became supported by the Christian lobby in the US. The interest and involvement of the US was due to the influence of American Evangelical Christians; according to Huliaras (2008, 163), this group of Christians took an interest in Sudan as they considered the Muslims of the North to be

---

[5] A detailed discussion of the difference between achieving peace and achieving justice is outside the scope of this chapter.
[6] An analysis of the legitimacy of South Sudan following secession is outside the scope of this chapter as the chapter is concerned with the current attitude of the UN towards membership of secessionist states rather than the aftermath of secession.

persecuting Christians in the South). It was due to their influence that the US became more involved in the Sudanese peace process, and 'under strong pressure from Washington, Khartoum and the rebels finally reached an agreement in Machakos, Kenya that acknowledged the right of the Southern Sudanese to self-determination' (Huliaras 2008, 171–172). This went on to develop into the CPA, which, at the behest of the United States, included the provision of a referendum for South Sudanese independence to be held in 2011 (Copeland 2013, 26).

From this it can be seen that the internal workings of third-party states, particularly democratic, powerful states, have a considerable impact on the likelihood that a secessionist movement will receive official recognition. This in turn shows how the recognition of secession can be affected by powerful states' self-interest. From a UN perspective it is worth noting that the US would be less likely to use its Security Council veto right to block admission of a new state if the admission of said state was in the US interest.

As previously seen in this chapter, whilst the UN Charter ostensibly supports self-determination, it cannot be interpreted as a general right to secede due to the detrimental effect such a precedent would have on the international system of states as we know it. However, the granting of recognition to the independence of South Sudan can be justified morally both as an act of remedial secession, upholding R2P and as an act of conflict resolution. Although, as will be seen in the next case study, the same pragmatism and principle is not always employed by the international community and does not always lead to accession to the UN leading to an argument that the UN only supports remedial secession from failed states in cases of *ongoing* civil war.[7]

Case Study: Somaliland

Somaliland is a secessionist state in the north of Somalia that does not have a seat in the UNGA, nor is it recognised by any UN member state. Somalia itself is the archetypal Weberian failed state. It has been without an effective government, at least in terms of providing security for its citizens, since the fall of Siad Barre in 1991 and groups around the country control various regions, meaning that the Mogadishu government does not have the monopoly on the use of force (Stremlau 2019). It topped the *Foreign Policy/ Fund for Peace* failed/fragile states index from 2008–13 and has been ranked in the top two to date (Fund For Peace 2018). In the north of the country there is a secessionist entity known as Somaliland, which has been shown to have

---

[7] For the purposes of studying the UN attitude to secession from failed states, the post-independence conflict within South Sudan will not be considered as it is outside the scope of the chapter.

its own functioning democratic government (Stremlau 2019).

Somaliland arguably fits the criteria for remedial secession under the auspices of R2P. This is due to the Mogadishu government not upholding its side of the social contract in so much as it is unable to provide security to its citizens. This is illustrated by the Somali government not being in control of the majority of its territory, Somaliland included, for decades and therefore being unable to protect its citizens from atrocities (such as attacks by Al-Shabaab) or to provide basic security. This is compounded by the fact that there have been reports of government forces raping, murdering and looting Somali citizens, the looting being attributed to the fact that these forces were often not paid by the government and are therefore forced to rely on looting for survival, further undermining the legitimacy of the Somali government (Hanson and Kaplan 2008). Further to this, the Federal Government of Somalia (formerly Transitional Federal Government) is not representative of Somaliland. Whilst the Somali Government claims Somaliland as a federal entity within a united Somalia, the Issaq clan (the dominant clan in Somaliland), have so far refused to participate, meaning that the Somali government cannot claim to have 'a government representing the whole people belonging to the territory' as expressed in UNGA Resolution 2625(XXV). Somaliland's lack of UN membership could possibly refute the earlier point about the violation of UNGA Resolution 2625(XXV) being a catalyst to UN membership for a remedial secession.

One could argue that this discrepancy is due to the fact that the citizens of Somaliland are not an ethnic minority, however it can be argued that the Isaaq clan is still a distinct group within Somalia that have suffered past persecution and discrimination at the hands of the central government, as this chapter will see, and the current recognised government of Somalia is incapable of protecting this group from future persecution. As such, in this case at least, the desired quality for a government to be 'representing the whole people belonging to the territory' as UNGA Resolution 2625(XXV) stipulates, does not necessarily refer to ethnic minorities alone.

Importantly, an overwhelming majority (97%) of the population of Somaliland voted in favour of the constitution, which reaffirmed support for independence (Farley 2011). As seen in the South Sudan, referendum supporting independence among other factors, which combined with a lack of legitimacy of the parent state, led to recognition and UN membership. Yet this has not been the case with Somaliland. This shows a major inconsistency in the attitudes of the UN and its members towards secession from failed states when looking at this particular set of factors. The difference here is that the secession of Somaliland is not causing conflict on the scale of the Sudanese

Civil War.[8] It can even be said that Somaliland is a victim of its success now, its relative stability and peaceful existence mean that it can be more easily ignored by the wider international community (Keating 2018). Geldenhuys (2009, 139) elaborates on this, stating that 'its peace and stability amid the turmoil of Somalia did not capture media headlines or arouse humanitarian concerns'. This also shows that when self-determination through secession from failed states is condoned in the UN, it is linked to the UN's role as a peacemaker. It also shows that secession attempts, even when not recognised by anyone, can lead to a relatively stable and peaceful co-existence. The UN role in the conflict mediation in the Sudanese Civil War showed that such negotiations can lead to self-determination through secession. However, if there is no major conflict to mediate, then it appears unlikely that a secession from a failed state will achieve UN membership, as the case of Somaliland illustrates.

Another somewhat anomalous feature about Somaliland's lack of UN membership is that the secessionist claim of Somaliland is based upon the original colonial border between British Somaliland and Italian Somalia. Indeed, Somaliland had briefly been a separate nation following decolonisation and prior to a union with Somalia a matter of days later. Thus, Somaliland's claim for independence could be seen as the dissolution of a union rather than a unilateral secession, and so fears over setting a precedent that could undermine the international norm of territorial integrity should be less of a concern. This is because it will be a reversion to previous borders rather than creating new ones, as has previously been accepted by the international community in cases such as the dissolution of the USSR, the breakup of Czechoslovakia and Yugoslavia. It seems there is something of an inconsistency here in how secessionist states in post-colonial Africa have gained UN membership. Post-colonial secessions such as Eritrea and, as we have seen, South Sudan have gained UN membership, yet Somaliland has not. One can argue that this is due to the oppression that the Eritreans and South Sudanese faced at the hands of their respective parent states, giving them the right to remedial secession under the auspices of R2P. However, Somaliland has a similar claim due to the persecution the Isaaq clan faced under the presidency of Barre. For example, according to Worthington (2004), opposition to Barre's rule amongst the Issaq had been met with:

> [T]he extraordinary situation in which Barre's aircraft would take off from Hargeysa [sic] airport, bomb and strafe the city, load up again at the airport and carry on. They continued until

---

[8] Whilst the Somali civil war is ongoing and was a factor which led to Somaliland's secession, the secession itself is not causing a highly destructive war on the scale of that in Sudan (border skirmishes with neighbouring Puntland notwithstanding).

there were 50,000 dead in Hargeysa and hundreds of thousands of dead in the rest of Somaliland...the rest of the population fled. That was the most extreme attempt at genocide against the dominant Isaq [sic] clan.

However, related to the aforementioned point about Somaliland's current relative peaceful existence, the fact that there is no ongoing, highly destructive conflict specifically regarding the secession of Somaliland can explain a lack of UN mediation on the issue and be a possibility as to why Somaliland has yet to achieve UN membership. However, the Mogadishu government remains both unrepresentative of Somaliland and unable to uphold security in the region. Importantly, Somaliland has proven to be relatively secure, even showing the beginnings of democracy, having held a number of elections and being classified as 'partly free' and an 'emerging democracy' by Thinktank Freedom House (Keating 2018). This means that Mogadishu's claim on Somaliland can be seen as illegitimate based on both UNGA Resolution 2625(XXV) and R2P.

Analysis

In the case of the secession of South Sudan it was an apparent lack of legitimacy of the parent state that allowed the secessionists passage to UN accession based around UNGA Resolution 2625(XXV) (Brown 2018, 227–229; Gettleman 2011). In addition to this, when one considers the UN principle of R2P, it compounds the case for allowing UN membership based on the principle of remedial secession. However, it would seem that this is a case of principle justifying pragmatism, and that allowing a seat to remedial secessionists, from a failed state or otherwise, is the exception rather than the rule. We have seen that Somaliland remains unrecognised. This is despite having many similar features to the secession of South Sudan, in which the secessionists succeeded in becoming UN members. Such features include, being unrepresented in its parent state, having suffered oppression at the hands of the state and holding the balance of legitimacy over its parent state based on these factors, plus the parent state's inability to govern.

Whilst conflict resolution can be seen to have played a part in the admission of South Sudan to the UN, it must be noted that even in cases of conflict resolution secessionist states have not necessarily been admitted to the UN; an example of this would be South Ossetia and Abkhazia. An analysis of these conflicts is outside the scope of this chapter; however, it is important to note that the interests of the global powers, most notably the P-5, have a great bearing on whether new states become UN members. For example, the secession of Abkhazia and South Ossetia was opposed by NATO (2008), of which the US, France and the UK are members. The interests of these countries in opposing this secession is shown by the fact that the parent state in question, Georgia, is a prospective member of NATO (2019). This illustrates that the self-interest of states, particularly those on the P-5, can hinder a secessionist state's hopes of becoming a UN member. Likewise, support of a powerful patron-state (along with a lack of opposition from other powerful states) can increase the likelihood of a state gaining recognition. This was seen in the US support for the independence of South Sudan. Conversely it would appear that the secession of Somaliland is largely inconsequential to the global powers.

As previously mentioned, it is not the UN that recognises states as such, but grants membership based on the recognition of its member states; however, its member states can, ostensibly, use UN principles such as the UN Charter, UNGA Resolution 2625(XXV) and R2P, as supported in the UN resolution following the 2005 World Summit Outcome, in order to inform their decision to recognise a secessionist state. It would seem that it is in the general interest of states to uphold the primacy of territorial integrity, even in cases where a secession is causing conflict. These principles that can be interpreted to support remedial secession from a failed state are only interpreted as such in cases where pragmatic conflict resolution is combined with recent oppression of the people of the secessionist state. They are also only interpreted as such when the secession in question does not go against the interests of the P5. This is in order to uphold the international states system as we know it. This chapter will conclude by assessing how appropriate this stance is.

Conclusions

The UN line on self-determination through secession is such that secessionist states are unlikely to gain membership as the principle of territorial integrity holds primacy, which initially would show it to be a foe to self-determination through secession. However, as has been seen in cases such as South Sudan, the principle of territorial integrity is not absolute and has limits, most notably when the parent state is not fulfilling its side of the social contract by failing to provide security for its citizens. However, so far, the UN has not voiced support for the admission of secessionist states without the consent of the parent state (Orakhelashvili 2008, 8). This has sometimes been as part of a peace settlement, such as in the case of South Sudan, and if the failure of the parent state to provide security is down to direct oppression and persecution that is an ongoing concern. The principle of allowing these exceptions to the primacy of territorial integrity can be linked to UNGA Resolutions 545(VI) and 2625(XXV) and R2P, which would show the UN to be a friend to self-determination through secession in this instance. However, there is an argument, as noted in the introduction, that cases of *passive* failure to provide basic security and rights. This was evident in the case of Somalia, as illustrated by the aforementioned inability of the Somali government to prevent its forces raping and looting. This can invoke the same principles. The fact that Somaliland is not a UN member would show the UN to be a foe to self-determination through secession in this instance.

As previously noted, the settlements that saw South Sudan become recognised were part of a negotiation for the resolution of conflict between the secessionists and their parent state. This indicates that the eventual admission of these states to the UN was a pragmatic move in order to create stability in the respective regions. This pragmatism can be further morally justified by the remedial right to secede and R2P, and its legitimacy justified by caveats such as UNGA Resolution 2625(XXV). However, arguably it would be just as pragmatic and moral to allow Somaliland to join the UN. It can be seen as compensation for the past wrongs of Barre, as well as promoting stability in at least part of Somalia, a country that is otherwise a failed state. This inconsistency can be explained since, as noted, Somaliland itself is not a major international security concern and thus does not warrant UN mediation in negotiations that could lead to recognition and UN membership. It was also not in the interests of any of the P-5 to recognise; both of these factors are in contrast to the case of South Sudan. Thus, keeping a somewhat ambiguous approach allows the UN to admit new members in cases of pressing threats to international security such as ongoing conflict, yet prevents a mass proliferation of states that could undermine the international states system, and also allows the P-5 to uphold their interests.

The issue of state failure has been observed to be taken into account by the UN in the case of South Sudan. Thus, ostensibly one could argue that the UN is a friend to self-determination via secession if the balance of legitimacy is tipped towards the secessionists. However, the fact that Somaliland is not yet a UN member can be argued to refute this observation, thus it could be argued that the lack of legitimacy of a parent state and potential increased legitimacy of the secessionist state is only taken into account in cases of a pragmatic response to conflict resolution and when such secession does not contravene the interests of the P-5. The case of South Sudan showed that the UN can be a friend to self-determination through secession in the context of state failure when required to facilitate mediation of conflict resolution that may result in secession (possibly at the behest of a major power). In such an incidence UN resolutions and principles can be interpreted as supporting such secessions, so long as none of the P-5 object. However, the UN is a foe to self-determination through secession in the context of state failure when there is not an immediate security threat and such a secession is not supported by a major P-5 power, as Somaliland has shown. This, however, fits in with the principle of territorial integrity which is a major principle of the UN and supported throughout the international community as it prevents a precedent that could undermine the international system of states. This means that the UN being a friend to self-determination via secession, even in the case of secession from failed states, is the exception rather than the rule.

References

Anaya, James S. 1996. *Indigenous Peoples in International Law.* New York: Oxford University Press.

Aust, Anthony. 2005. *Handbook of International Law*. Cambridge: Cambridge University Press.

BBC. 2011. "South Sudan referendum: 99% vote for independence." *BBC*, January 30, 2011.
http://www.bbc.co.uk/news/world-africa-12317927.

Brown, Edmund. 2018. "Secession from Failed States: Ethical and Practical Issues with Current Approaches." Ph.D. diss., University of Leicester.

Buchanan, Allen. 1997. "Theories of Secession." *Philosophy and Public Affairs* 26(1): 31–61.

Buchanan, Allen. 2004. *Justice, Legitimacy and Self-Determination: Moral Foundations for International Law.* New York: Oxford University Press.

Copeland, Eddie. 2013. "New State Formation: The Case of South Sudan." MA diss., University of Leicester.

Eckert, Amy E. 2002. "Constructing States: The Role of the International Community in the Creation of New States." *Journal of Public and International Affairs* 13: 19–39.

Farley, Ben. 2001. "Recognition of Somaliland Overdue." *World Politics Review*, January 26, 2011.
http://www.worldpoliticsreview.com/articles/7673/recognition-of-somaliland-overdue.

Fund For Peace. 2018. "Fragile States Index 2018." Accessed August 13, 2018. http://fundforpeace.org/fsi/data/.

Fund For Peace. 2019. *Fragile States Index: Annual Report 2019*. Washington D.C.: The Fund for Peace. http://fundforpeace.org/wp-content/uploads/2019/04/9511904-fragilestatesindex.pdf.

Geldenhuys, Deon. 2009. *Contested States in World Politics*. London: Palgrave Macmillan.

Hanson, Stephanie, and Eben Kaplan. 2008. "Somalia's Transitional Government." *Council on Foreign Relations*, May 12, 2008. http://www.cfr.org/somalia/somalias-transitional-government/p12475.

Huliaras, Asteris. 2008. "The Evangelical Roots of US Africa Policy." *Survival* 50(6): 161–182.

Janik, Ralph. 2013. "The Responsibility to Protect as an Impetus for Secessionist Movements: On the Necessity to Re-Think Territorial Integrity." In *Grenzen im Völkerrecht*, edited by Matthias Kettemann, 41–69. Vienna: Jan Sramek Verlag.

Keating, Joshua. 2018. "When is a nation not a nation: Somaliland's dream of independence." *The Guardian*, July 20, 2018. https://www.theguardian.com/news/2018/jul/20/when-is-a-nation-not-a-nation-somalilands-dream-of-independence.

Kuperman, Alan J. 2009. "Rethinking the Responsibility to Protect." *The Whitehead Journal of Diplomacy and International Relations* 10(1): 19–29.

Montevideo Convention on the Rights and Duties of States, Montevideo, December 26, 1933, *United Nations Treaty Series*, 165(3802): 19–45, available from https://treaties.un.org/doc/Publication/UNTS/LON/Volume%20165/v165.pdf.

NATO. 2008. "Statement by the North Atlantic Council on the Russian Recognition of South Ossetia and Abkhazia regions of Georgia." Last updated August 22, 2009. http://www.nato.int/cps/en/natohq/news_43517.htm?selectedLocale=en.

NATO. 2019. "Enlargement." Last updated February 15, 2019. https://www.nato.int/cps/en/natohq/topics_49212.htm.

Orakhelashvili, Alexander. "Statehood, Recognition and the United Nations System: A Unilateral Declaration of Independence in Kosovo." In *Max Planck Yearbook of United Nations Law*, edited by A. Armin von Bogdandy and Rudiger Wolfrum, Volume 12, 1–144. https://www.mpil.de/files/pdf2/mpunyb_01_orakhel_12.pdf.

Pavkovic, Aleksandar, and Peter Radan. 2007. *Creating New States: Theory and Practice of Secession*. Aldershot: Ashgate.

Pellet, Alain. 1992. "The opinions of the Badinter Arbitration Committee: A Second Breath for the Self-Determination of Peoples." *European Journal of International Law* 3(1): 178–185.

Potter Donald. W. 2004. "State Responsibility, Sovereignty, and Failed States." Refereed paper presented to the Australasian Political Studies Association Conference, University of Adelaide, September 29–October 1, 2004, available from https://parlinfo.aph.gov.au/parlInfo/search/display/display.w3p;query=Id:%22media/pressrel/WS1F6%22.

Rich, Roland. 1993. "Recognition of States: The Collapse of Yugoslavia and the Soviet Union." *The European Journal of International Law* 38(4): 36–65.

Ryngaert, Cedric, and Nico Schrijver. 2015. "Lessons Learned from the Srebrenica Massacre: From UN Peacekeeping Reform to Legal Responsibility." *Netherlands International Review* (62)2: 219–227.

Sharkey, Heather J. 2008. "Arab Identity and Ideology in Sudan: The Politics of Language, Identity and Race." *African Affairs* 107(426): 21–43.

Stremlau, Nicole. 2019. "Governance Without Government in the Somali Territories." *Journal of International Affairs*, January 9, 2019. https://jia.sipa.columbia.edu/governance-without-government-somali-territories.

The Comprehensive Peace Agreement Between the Government of the Republic of the Sudan and the Sudan People's Liberation Movement/Sudan People's Liberation Army. *UNMIS*, January 9, 2005, Machakos Protocol. https://unmis.unmissions.org/sites/default/files/old_dnn/cpa-en.pdf.

UN Office on Genocide Prevention and the Responsibility to Protect. 2019. "Responsibility to Protect: About." Accessed October 2, 2019. https://www.un.org/en/genocideprevention/about-responsibility-to-protect.shtml.

UN Peacemaker. 1972. The Addis Ababa Agreement on the Problem of South Sudan. *UN Department of Political and Peacebuilding Affairs*, February 27, 1972. https://peacemaker.un.org/sites/peacemaker.un.org/files/SD_720312_Addis%20Ababa%20Agreement%20on%20the%20Problem%20of%20South%20Sudan.pdf.

United Nations. 1945. *Charter of the United Nations and the Statute of the International Court of Justice*. San Francisco: United Nations Press. https://treaties.un.org/doc/publication/ctc/uncharter.pdf.

United Nations. 1996. "The United Nations and Somalia 1992–1996" *The United Nations Blue Book Series* Volume VIII, New York: United Nations Publication.

United Nations. 2019. "About UN Membership." Accessed October 2, 2019. http://www.un.org/en/sections/member-states/about-un-membership/index.html.

United Nations, Department of Public Information, *Outreach Programme on the Rwanda Genocide and the United Nations: The Responsibility to Protect*. Background Note, March 2012, https://www.un.org/en/preventgenocide/rwanda/pdf/bgresponsibility.pdf.

United Nations, General Assembly, *Implementing the Responsibility to Protect: Report of the Secretary General*, A/63/677 (12 January 2009), available from https://www.undocs.org/en/A/63/677.

United Nations General Assembly Resolution 545(VI), *Inclusion in the International Covenant or Covenants on Human Rights of an article relating to the Right of Peoples to Self-Determination*, A/RES/545(VI) (5 February 1952), available from https://undocs.org/en/A/RES/545(VI).

United Nations General Assembly Resolution 1514(XV), *Declaration on the Granting of Independence to Colonial Countries and Peoples,* A/RES/1514(XV) (14 December 1960), available from https://www.undocs.org/en/A/RES/1514(XV).

United Nations General Assembly Resolution 2625(XXV), *Declaration on Principles of International Law concerning Friendly Relations and Co-operation among States in accordance with the Charter of the United Nations*, A/RES/*2625*(XXV) (24 October 1970), available from https://www.undocs.org/en/ A/RES/2625(XXV).

United Nations General Assembly Resolution 60/1, *2005 World Summit Outcome*, A/RES/60/1 (16 September 2005), available from https://www.undocs.org/en/A/RES/60/1.

United Nations Mission in Sudan. 2005. The Comprehensive Peace Agreement Between the Government of the Republic of the Sudan and the Sudan People's Liberation Movement/Sudan People's Liberation Army. UNMIS, January 9, 2005, Machakos Protocol. https://unmis.unmissions.org/sites/default/files/old_dnn/cpa-en.pdf.

Weber, Max. 1919. *Politics as a Vocation*. Available from: http://anthropos-lab.net/wp/wp-content/uploads/2011/12/Weber-Politics-as-a-Vocation.pdf.

Weller Marc. 1992. "The International Response to the Dissolution of the Socialist Federal Republic of Yugoslavia" *The American Journal of International Law* 86(3): 569–607.

Woodward, Peter. 1990. *Sudan 1898–1989: The Unstable State*. Boulder: Lynne Rienner Publishers Inc.

Worthington, Tony. 2004. "Statement on Somaliland." *Westminster Hall Debates* Vol. 417, Part No. 534, Column 273WH, February 4, 2004. http://www.publications.parliament.uk/pa/cm200304/cmhansrd/vo040204/halltext/40204h03.htm.

7

Self-Determination as Resistance: Sahrawi and Palestinian Struggle for the UN

MOARA ASSIS CRIVELENTE

This chapter[1] draws on the cases of Western Sahara and Palestine to begin exploring the United Nations' (UN) role in realising the peoples' right to self-determination. It addresses the UN's role in conflicts perceived by actors as protracted due to its lack of resolve, due to manipulation by world powers and due to the 'international community's lack of political will', as diplomats, parliamentarians, party cadres and activists said in almost every interview conducted for this research.[2] Considering Sahrawis' and Palestinians' growing scepticism, but also how they continue to claim the fulfilment of the self-determination promise by and through the UN, I address their persistence as resistance conducted through continuing participation.

The parallel does not imply that both cases are identical. Still, they share many attributes and goals, beginning with their characterisation as struggles for self-determination against protracted foreign occupation and colonisation. The chapter starts by sketching a conceptualisation of self-determination and its development. The first part discusses the concept's development and the

---

[1] This piece is part of ongoing research; its topic is certainly not exhausted here. Many aspects of the discussion on self-determination, the UN's limits and the cases addressed had to be left out, for now. I wish to express my sincere gratitude for the editor's invaluable comments and amendments to the initial draft and, as per usual, state that remaining flaws are my own responsibility.

[2] Interviews with civil society actors, diplomats and other officials from Western Sahara, Palestine and other countries, as well as participant observation of side events in the UN Human Rights Council were conducted in 2017–2018. Quotations are included here with the sources' consent.

second overviews UN approaches to both cases, addressing Palestinian and Sahrawi expectations and action. It briefly contextualises the cases within a colonial framework sustained by a significant asymmetry and structured by Israel's and Morocco's enduring military occupation of Palestine and Western Sahara respectively. The conclusion reflects on how resistance to negligence and manipulation translates into a struggle for the very UN, for its promises and, ultimately, for liberation.

A Developing Principle or an Accommodating Promise?

The conceptualisation of self-determination has long advanced according to international dynamics. This section offers a non-exhaustive chronology exemplifying debates on the peoples' freedom from foreign domination and freedom to choose their own political systems based on national and territorial claims, which have promoted the right of self-determination. Many genealogies identify Woodrow Wilson's *Fourteen Points* speech as the principle's liberal parent, but neglect debates with which Karl Marx, Friedrich Engels, Vladimir Lenin, Rosa Luxembourg and others engaged, and the role of peoples' struggles in pushing for the principle's development (Cassese 1995; Bowring 2008). For instance, for Bowring (2008, 9), the right of peoples to self-determination, 'the most significant gain of post-World War II international law', was 'welded' to it 'in the context of the Russian Revolution, in theoretical and practical struggles'. Although the latter is the reading my research builds on, this section deals with self-determination within the UN framework.

The 1945 UN Charter defines self-determination as essential for strengthening universal peace in Chapter I, while Chapter XI sets the framework for decolonisation. In 1960, in a period of intensifying anti-colonial struggle, UN General Assembly (UNGA) Resolution 1514(XV) adopted the Declaration on the Granting of Independence to Colonial Countries and Peoples, referring to principles of national unity and territorial integrity. The Declaration brings important points to the UN register. It deems the process of liberation 'irresistible and irreversible' and argues for an end to colonialism 'and all practices of segregation and discrimination associated therewith' in order to 'avoid serious crises'. It also declares that alien subjugation, domination and exploitation of peoples violates their human rights and the UN Charter's principles, preventing 'the promotion of world peace and cooperation'.

However, discussion on whether self-determination was indeed graduated from a political principle into a legal right, or when that happened, is ongoing. Laing (1992) argues that, through a 'humanitarian universalism', the 1941

Atlantic Charter issued by U.S. President Franklin Roosevelt and British Prime Minister Winston Churchill – later endorsed by others in the 1942 Declaration of the United Nations – establishes the *norm* of self-determination. Three years before the signing of the UN Charter, the Declaration by the United Nations 'pledged the signatory governments to the maximum war effort and bound them against making a separate peace' (United Nations 1942). Bowring (2008) argues that the right is defined as such in common Article I of the 1966 international covenants on civil and political rights and on economic, social, and cultural rights (ICCPR and ICESCR). The article states: 'All peoples have the right of self-determination', they may 'freely determine their political status and freely pursue their economic, social and cultural development', as well as 'freely dispose of their natural wealth and resources'. It also declares that all state parties to the Covenants shall promote the realisation of the right of self-determination and respect that right.

Moreover, self-determination is usually defined by three categories: a) that of colonial peoples, b) that of secession, and c) that of groups demanding recognition or collective rights within states (Archibugi 2003). Respect for the diversity of democratic systems 'as important element for the promotion and protection of human rights', urged for in a report adopted by UNGA Resolution 60/164 (2005), has also been promoted. Some still argue that self-determination cannot be concluded in one historical event and must be considered a process, 'subject to revision and adjustment', one that 'cannot be understood as a one-time choice (...) because, like the rights to life, freedom and identity, it is too fundamental to be waived', as put by Alfred-Maurice de Zayas (Office of the High Commissioner for Human Rights 2014, 3). This line of argument raises concerns with a relativization of *certain* sovereignty, national unity and territorial integrity and the instrumentalization of conflicts by regional and world powers. An example is the secession of the Serbian province of Kosovo and Metohija, aided by the 1999 military intervention of the North Atlantic Treaty Organization (NATO) against the Federal Republic of Yugoslavia. This operation was an aggressive act (Jovanovic 2019) and a violation of the UN Charter (Momtaz 2000).[3]

Authors regarding the 'revolutionary and unclear character' of self-determination (Koskenniemi 1994, 241) or arguing for its historical recovery as an achievement of struggle (Bowring 2008) scrutinise its provenance, operationalization and emancipatory potential. I engage with the cases of Palestine and Western Sahara, and am concerned with the kind of struggle

---

[3] A resolution on the crime of aggression was adopted at the 2010 plenary meeting of the International Criminal Court in the framework of the Kampala Review Conference of the Rome Statute (International Criminal Court 2010).

through which the principle and right of self-determination is fought for. Hence, I draw from works focused on the role of resistance in the historical development of international law such as those of Cassese (1995), Rajagopal (2003), Bowring (2008), among others. This perspective supports my approach to struggles conducted within an institution said to be *the* promoter of self-determination (the UN), while considering that this being a *struggle* shows that the right of self-determination is disputed depending on the cases at hand, as discussed ahead.

The UN Approach to the 'Right of Peoples' from Palestine and Western Sahara

Colonial historical continuity is manifest in the cases of Palestine and Western Sahara.[4] Persistence in conducting liberation struggles through international institutions and legal instruments appears to reflect resistance to a historical closure that leaves people behind. But the variation in UN approaches to different cases shows how politically charged disputes are. Susan Akram (2014, 78) engages in this discussion by addressing the reasons for change in a territory's status, with emphasis on military occupation and the lack of clarity in defining colonisation in Palestine and Western Sahara. She notes specifically the UN's inability to enforce the prohibition of territorial aggression, prolonged occupation, and settler implantation, which constitute 'major barriers' to the realisation of both Palestinian and Sahrawi self-determination. This section offers an overview of each case, showing how these peoples' recent histories were impacted by the UN.

Western Sahara was put under Spain's control at the 1884 Berlin Conference and has been listed by the UN special committee for decolonisation as a non-self-governing territory since 1963.[5] In 1965, the General Assembly requested that Spain 'take immediately all necessary measures for the liberation' of the territory through UNGA Resolution A/2072 of 1965, and repeatedly urged the administering power to organise a referendum on self-determination. Confrontation ensued against the Sahrawi liberation movement – organised in the Popular Front for the Liberation of Saguía el-Hamra and Río de Oro (Polisario) in 1973. A UN mission of inquiry visited Western Sahara, Morocco, Mauritania and Algeria, reported that 'support for Polisario and for

---

[4] Colonialism or more specifically settler-colonialism has also been employed as a framework for discussing both cases; see for instance Khoury 2011, Zunes and Mundy 2015, Greenstein 2016, and for the conceptualisation of settler colonialism, see Wolfe 1999 and Veracini 2010.

[5] Western Sahara features at the top of the UN list at: www.un.org/en/decolonization/nonselfgovterritories.shtml.

independence in Western Sahara was widespread and recommend[ed] the holding of a referendum for self-determination' (Fadel 1999). The mission was requested by the UN General Assembly in the same resolution where it requested the advisory opinion of the International Court of Justice (A/RES/3292(XXIX) 13 December 1974). Spain first resisted, then accepted the consultation, starting preparations by conducting a census, but Morocco and Mauritania rejected it (ibid.). This was among the first chapters of ineffective UN attempts.

Spain left the territory in 1975 without organising the referendum, questionably transferring control to Morocco and Mauritania. Secret negotiations resulted in the 1975 Madrid Agreements, which does not legally mean that Spain's responsibility as an administering power was thus transferred (Zoubir 2007, 162; Ojeda-García et al. 2017). Polisario declared the Sahrawi Arab Democratic Republic (SADR) in 1976 and Mauritania abandoned its claims in 1979, while Morocco stayed in the territory, claiming that it was part of the kingdom before Spanish colonisation. However, a 1975 advisory opinion of the International Court of Justice (ICJ) did not find enough evidence supporting Morocco's claim and reaffirmed the Sahrawi people's right to self-determination (International Court of Justice 1975). Morocco interprets the opinion as favourable to the kingdom's claim over Western Sahara, thus justifying invasion, annexation of and settlement in the territory (Zartman 2014, 60). Armed conflict dragged on for almost two decades.

Through the UN and the Organisation of African Unity's facilitation, a settlement plan established the 1991 cease-fire and 'the holding of a referendum without military or administrative constraints to enable the people of Western Sahara to choose between independence and integration with Morocco'.[6] It also established the UN Mission for the Referendum in Western Sahara (MINURSO), tasked with organising the consultation. The first deadline was January 1992, but the referendum was repeatedly postponed, until it disappeared from sight (Fadel 1999; Zunes and Mundy 2010). Partial proposals to revive the process, presented by the UN Secretary-General's personal envoy James Baker in 2001 and 2003 and Morocco's 2007 Autonomy Plan to grant Western Sahara autonomy have downplayed or neglected commitments with a referendum that could include independence as an option (Zartman 2014, 66–67). Despite essentially limiting self-determination to autonomy from the outset, Morocco's plan was praised for 'serious and credible efforts' by the UN Security Council and representatives from the US, France, Mali, and others (Morocco World News 2018).

---

[6] For records of the plans, see the UN Security Council report at: www.un.org/en/sc/repertoire/89-92/Chapter%208/AFRICA/item%2008_Western%20Sahara_.pdf.

As for Palestine, the UN has grappled with the question since its own establishment. With the end of World War I and the fall of the Ottoman Empire, the United Kingdom and France divided the Levant. Soon, the nascent League of Nations established a Mandate System, putting Palestine under British administration, from the 1920s to 1948. The socioeconomic impacts on Arab inhabitants of colonisation and massive immigration bred growing conflicts, and the British administration tried to appease both Arabs and the Zionist movement (Halliday 1972; Masalha 2003; Said 2003; Pappé 2006). Variations of a partition plan were promoted until the UNGA adopted one, through Resolution 181, in 1947, even though most of the Arabs rejected the proposal, which they saw as continuing colonisation (Jamal 2005; Saleh 2014). While the Mandate System did little towards decolonisation, being what Akram (2014, 76) describes a 'compromise between the notion of self-determination and the interests of the colonial powers', when the League was dissolved, some territories were put under the UN Trusteeship System and have either achieved independence or association with other states. However, when the British Mandate ended and the State of Israel was declared, in 1948, Palestine's question was not transferred to UN Trusteeship but to a Special Committee on Palestine (UNSCOP). War ensued leaving around 15,000 Palestinians dead and about 500 villages destroyed, driving more than 700,000 to seek refuge in neighbouring villages or countries, creating an enduring 'refugee problem' (Masalha 1992, 2003; Said 2003; Pappé 2006). Refugees are since assisted by the UN Relief and Works Agency for Palestine Refugees in the Near East (UNRWA), created in 1949. Other confrontations between Israel and Arab countries had direct impact on the question of Palestine, which explains the agency's growing challenges. in 2018, six million Palestinian refugees and dependants were registered for assistance (UNRWA 2019), a situation that endures despite the refugees' widely recognised right of return, as stated in UNGA Resolution 194(III) of 1948.

In 1964 the Palestinian Liberation Organisation (PLO) was established, soon confronting Israel through armed action and initially classified as a terrorist organisation. In the 1967 War, Israel occupied the West Bank, Gaza Strip and other Arab territories that remain under its control, and focus shifted to the occupying power's responsibilities toward the people's protection under the unclearly defined 'temporary condition' of an occupation that became prolonged (Tilley 2012; Jabarin 2013).[7] The conflict's framework has been that of international humanitarian law, but due to the protraction of such a

---

[7] The 1907 Hague Regulations and 1949 Fourth Geneva Convention outline the occupying powers' obligations and the practices that constitute war crimes in that supposedly temporary situation. Article 42 of the Hague Regulations defines that 'a territory is considered occupied when it is actually placed under the authority of the hostile army.'

situation and the practices and policies sustaining it, looking at it as colonialism seems inevitable. After having affirmed the Palestinian people's inalienable *national rights* in Resolution 3236 (1974), the UNGA subsequently invited the PLO, as the representative of the Palestinian people, 'to participate in the efforts for peace in the Middle East', in Resolution 3375 (1975).

Concerned with the situation's protraction, that same year the UNGA established the UN Committee on the Exercise of the Inalienable Rights of the Palestinian People (CEIRPP). It was mandated with advising the UNGA on a programme to realise the Palestinians' 'right to self-determination without external interference, the right to national independence and sovereignty, and the right to return to their homes and property from which they have been displaced', and expressed concern that 'no just solution to the problem of Palestine has yet been achieved' (UNGA Resolution 3376). The mandate has been renewed annually, which reflects how the situation has dragged on. In the 1990s, mutual recognition between Israelis and Palestinians paved the way for the Oslo Agreements, which should have led to the State of Palestine's independence. However, the territory fragmented and became increasingly populated by Israeli settlers in colonies mainly built on expropriated land. Palestinian institutions became deeply dependent on foreign and Israeli funding, while the people remained under an omnipresent Israeli military occupation, in refugee camps or exile. The result was an ever-deeper discontentment with the peace process (Said 2001; Shlaim 2005; Khalidi 2006).

Sahrawis and Palestinians share many aspects in their struggles for self-determination. They both face a diplomatic dead-end favouring the occupying powers, which benefit from world powers' support, and seek a way out of a colonising status quo. For instance, the United States has repeatedly prioritised Israeli over Palestinian concerns while declaring itself a mediator, financed Israel's military and declared that it would continue to veto UN Security Council resolutions contrary to Israel's interests (White House 2015). However, their cases have different places in the UN. Western Sahara is listed as a non-self-governing territory, has its claim mainly dealt with by the Decolonisation Committee, and has a UN mission in place. Palestine is not on the decolonisation list: its case is dealt with through dedicated committees and agencies and has its right to a state clearly affirmed since the UN establishment. When addressing Palestine, the UN Secretary-General's 2017 Report on UN activities relating to self-determination (A/72/317) recalls that '[t]he right of the Palestinian people to self-determination, including the right to their independent State of Palestine, was reaffirmed by the General Assembly in its Resolution 71/184.'

Since the 1960s, the Sahrawis' general will for independence has been recognised (Fadel 1999; Zunes and Mundy 2010), but this option has been missing from recent calls for negotiated settlement (Roussellier 2014). For instance, in contrast with Palestine's case, which is dealt with in a dedicated section, the same 2017 Secretary-General Report addresses UNGA activities on Western Sahara in the Non-Self-Governing Territories section. The text expresses support for negotiations initiated by the Security Council 'to achieve a just, lasting and *mutually acceptable* political solution, which would provide for the self-determination of the people of Western Sahara'. Further, the report welcomes the parties' 'commitment to continue to show political will and work in an atmosphere propitious for dialogue, in order to enter into a more intensive phase of negotiations, in good faith and without preconditions' (A/72/317).

The State of Palestine was recognised by over 130 countries and by the UNGA in 2012 as an observer non-member state, but its territory and people remain under occupation. The SADR was recognised by over 80 countries and is a member of the African Union (AU) but has a decolonisation process pending. Despite protraction and frustration, Palestinians and Sahrawis demand commitment with UN principles. They resist a stagnation that enables the continuing colonisation of their territories, each facing opponents that count on diplomatic and financial support mainly from the US, the UK and France (Ojeda-García et al. 2017; Khalidi 2006). There is a clear vision laid out by Palestinian and Sahrawi actors of how political their struggle is, a perspective that informs their strategies, bent on exposing colonial lineages and structures.

Conditional Self-Determination

Recently, UNGA Resolution 72/159 (2017) stated 'firm opposition to acts of foreign military intervention, aggression and occupation', which result 'in the suppression of the right of peoples to self-determination and other human rights in certain parts of the world'. Still, the UN has not remedied these instances; protraction has fed into direct conflicts and colonisation, while self-determination becomes an obstacle or a complex variable to be considered in policies and diplomatic strategies. Morocco argues that it defends territorial integrity, even though the kingdom's claim over Western Sahara is unsubstantiated, as the ICJ stated in 1975. Security, in both Morocco's and Israel's cases, is also presented as a strategic concern protracting the actualisation of self-determination; it is also often used to justify the multifaceted control exercised by the occupying powers over people's lives and territory (Turner 2015; Halper 2015), systematic repression and even military offensives. Carlos Ruiz Miguel (2001, 344) argues that political manoeuvres and attempts at ignoring the Sahrawi people's right challenges the very evolution of international law. He questions whether this right to self-determination can be replaced by a political arrangement not contemplated by any law, and whether a people's statehood can be disputed while a referendum for self-determination is still pending (ibid). The notion that the form of the conflict's end, however recognised the right of self-determination, is up for negotiation is found in UN resolutions and diplomatic attempts, which raises concerns of the fact that self-determination itself is relative (ibid.; Becker 1998).

Human rights are key to the strategic frameworks of these struggles. Palestinians and Sahrawis, in interviews and reports, argue that the struggle for self-determination and human rights advocacy are the two faces of the same coin. Bowring (2008, 129) considers that human rights 'provide a ground for judgment, to the extent that they are understood in their historical context, and as, and to the extent to which, they embody and define the content of real human struggles'. Actors interviewed for this research and more denounce the effects of protracted colonisation and military occupation with human rights advocacy and complaints to UN mechanisms and special procedures. Interviews, my participant-observation in activities and analysis of campaign material, reports and publicised debates show that their strategies have taken dynamic forms, spurring, aided by these struggles' expansion and growing internationalisation, and also responding to their opponents' equally changing approaches.[8] Examples are campaigns against Moroccan exploitation and commercialisation of Sahrawi natural resources (Sahara Rise 2018), the Palestinian campaign for Boycott, Divestment and Sanctions (BDS), or the demand for a database to be released by the UN Office of the High Commissioner for Human Rights on companies that deal with Israeli settlements in Palestine (Al-Haq 2018).

Archibugi (2003, 488) argues that if the right of self-determination is 'self-assessed by conflicting political communities', and not 'precisely matched by a body of law', conflict outcomes 'will likely reflect the power of the contending parties rather than the interest of the peoples'. Advocating for a cosmopolitan legal order, he argues that self-determination 'should be fitted into a legal system far broader than that of single states or even that of interstates law' (2003, 489). Considering that such an order is not coming about soon, Archibugi suggests that 'independent third parties should assess the conflicting claims' (ibid.). However, could one expect that third parties do not

---

[8] Examples of publicized debates on strategy abound. For Palestine's case, see: 'Open forum: Strategizing Palestine' in *Journal of Palestine Studies* 35(3): 37–82; and for Western Sahara's case, see: 'Sahara Rise Manifest' in *Sahara Rise International Conference for Civil Resistance*, 25th to 27th February 2018.

project their own concerns onto cases, or that main parties accept opinions and/or judgements given by independent institutions such as courts or UN bodies? For instance, the 1975 ICJ Advisory Opinion on Western Sahara is disputed by Morocco, which interprets the piece's preamble as favourable to its claim, as mentioned before. As for Palestine, the reaction of Israel and the US to UN resolutions and reports is to claim that agencies, bodies or experts involved in their production have an anti-Israel bias (Ahren 2018). Moreover, despite its numerous resolutions and covenants seemingly granting peoples the right, as an international organisation, made of states guided by their respective foreign policies, the UN is clearly influenced by geopolitical considerations. Peoples struggling for self-determination understand that and do engage in these dynamics, while insisting on recovering what has historically been promoted as principled commitment, such as the right to self-determination.

Conclusions: Struggling for the UN

Fundamental issues outlined in this chapter include a perceived lack of definition of the subjects of the right to self-determination, questions regarding its status as a legal norm, its implementation and its stance in relation to principles such as territorial integrity and national unity. The first argument usually unfolds into two: how to define a 'people' and, considering specific cases of independence/liberation, how to demonstrate or justify historical claims over a territory. However, discussions along identity lines may work as deflection, keeping conflicts 'intractable', in which case the most powerful actors benefit from maintaining the *status quo*. Apparent vagueness and ambiguity keep disputes 'too complex' and are met with calls for compromise, as shown in the overview of Palestine and Western Sahara's cases, where their right to self-determination is put up for negotiation.

The UN has been perceived as unable or unwilling to make good on its promise. During the UN Special Committee on Decolonisation's session of June 2017, its Chair Rafael Darío Carreño (Venezuela) questioned the committee's relevance, stating that it is pervaded by a lack of interest in ending colonialism and lack of cooperation from administering and occupying powers.[9] Departing from the recognition of the Sahrawis' right to hold a referendum and adopting a strategy of denial after the 1991 cease-fire, as mentioned above, Morocco presented the 2007 Autonomy Plan previously mentioned, as if expressing good faith to rekindle negotiations, but removed the option for independence from the equation. Conditional self-determination becomes a concession from Morocco, which, as mentioned, is considered evidence of its 'serious and credible efforts' by UN bodies and world powers.

---

9   For more on the session, see: www.un.org/press/en/2017/gacol3311.doc.htm.

Participation and interaction with UN mechanisms and procedures vary according to challenges concerning access to the institution, which depends on accreditation and registration as non-governmental organisations according to state law.[10] By observing six sessions of the UN Human Rights Council (UNHRC) for two years and interviewing civil society actors there, I could list a few. For instance, the short time to speak at plenary sessions, the process undergone to get access to UN events, is a bureaucratic often prohibitive procedure given the limited resources available to civil society actors who face obstacles registering organisations and associations in the occupying states' systems. Obstacles such as fear of reprisals from these states for their work, or political dilemmas regarding the adoption of these states' legal frameworks, and much more. Still, people continue to participate, adopting diverse tactics to surpass such challenges, as Cheikha Abdalahe, a young Sahrawi advocate stated in a side event at a 2018 session of the UNHRC. On how to 'make it hard for them' just to have people disappear from history, Abdalahe stated:

> [World leaders] don't care about us, I am sure. What can we do? We have tens of thousands of people to defend. They give us time to speak here, about 1 minute and 30 seconds. But how can we talk about so many years of suffering in this time? This is a theatre, but we have a role to play here. So, let's play it right. [...] Are we wrong to believe in the UN? [...] They want us to disappear, but guess what, we will make it hard for them.[11]

Officials and activists interviewed from both Palestine and Western Sahara affirm that despite their commitment to diplomacy, self-determination is non-negotiable. After decades of waiting and being frustrated, some Sahrawis express concerns that some youth stopped believing in the international community's efforts and are ready, though not willing, to return to armed struggle. On the other hand, these actors state their resolve in 'claiming' international law and the very UN for the peoples' struggles. The problem is often said to be the monopolisation and manipulation of the main UN bodies by world powers with their stakes in these conflicts. Still, Palestinian and Sahrawi initiatives show historical but also ever broader engagement with instruments, mechanisms, mediation attempts, and in political action.

---

[10] To have consultative status with ECOSOC and get accreditation to participate in various agencies' events and procedures, organisations must apply and submit documents that include their certificate of registration issued by a governmental authority, see: http://csonet.org/?menu=34.

[11] Cheikha Abdalahe is a Sahrawi human rights activist living in Spain who frequently participates in many international fora. The statement that she made at the side event was written down by me and is reproduced here with her consent.

However, movements can be increasingly weary of the huge efforts made for slow or no progress, showing suspicion towards institutions and cynicism regarding the lack of political will from the 'international community' to recognise their claims, even though self-determination is a UN founding principle. Hence, the demanding of the fulfilment of that promise by the UN is one aspect of Sahrawi and Palestinian resistance to colonisation and is a refusal to waiver on rights fought for – and a refusal to waiver on the very UN itself.

References

Ahren, Raphael. 2018. "US quits the UN's Human Rights Council, citing its 'chronic bias against Israel.'" *The Times of Israel*, 20 June 2018. https://www.timesofisrael.com/us-quits-the-uns-human-rights-council-citing-its-chronic-bias-against-israel/.

Akram, Susan. 2014. "Self- Determination, Statehood, and the Refugee Question under International Law in Namibia, Palestine, Western Sahara, and Tibet." In *Still Waiting for Tomorrow: The Law and Politics of Unresolved Refugee Crises,* edited by Tom Syring and Susan Akram, 75–140. Boston: Cambridge Scholars Publishing.

Al-Haq. 2018. "Palestinian Organizations Support Release of UN Database Report and Call for Third State Action to End Corporate Complicity in Occupation." Accessed July 20, 2019. http://www.alhaq.org/advocacy/6280.html.

Archibugi, Daniele. 2003. "A Critical Analysis of the Self-determination of Peoples: A Cosmopolitan Perspective." *Constellations* 10(2): 488–505.

Becker, Tal. 1998. "Self-determination in Perspective: Palestinian Claims to Statehood and the Relativity of the Right to Self-determination." *Israel Law Review* 32(2): 301–354.

Bowring, Bill. 2008. *The Degradation of the International Legal Order? The Rehabilitation of Law and the Possibility of Politics.* New York: Routledge-Cavendish.

Cassese, Antonio. 1995. *Self-determination of Peoples: A legal reappraisal.* Cambridge: Cambridge University Press.

Dugard, John, and John Reynolds. 2013. "Apartheid, International Law, and the Occupied Palestinian Territory." *The European Journal of International Law* 24(3): 867–913.

Fadel, Kamal. 1999. "The decolonisation process in Western Sahara." *Indigenous Law Bulletin* 4, no. 23. Accessed January 15, 2019. http://classic.austlii.edu.au/au/journals/IndigLawB/1999/66.html.

Greenstein, Ran. 2016. "Settler Colonialism: A Useful Category of Historical Analysis?" *Jadaliyya*, 6 June 2016. Accessed September 20, 2019. https://www.jadaliyya.com/Details/33333/Settler-Colonialism-A-Useful-Category-of-Historical-Analysis.

Halliday, Fred. 1971. "On the PFLP and the September Crisis: Interview with Ghassan Kannafani." *New Left Review* 1(67): 50–57.

Halper, Jeff. 2015. *War against the people: Israel, the Palestinians and Global Pacification*. London: Pluto Press.

ICC. 2010. "ICC – Crime of Aggression, RC/Res.6." Accessed November 2, 2019.https://asp.icc-cpi.int/en_menus/asp/reviewconference/Pages/crime%20of%20aggression.aspx.

International Court of Justice, *Western Sahara: Advisory Opinion, ICJ Reports p. 12* (16 October 1975), available from icj-cij.org/files/case-related/61/061-19751016-ADV-01-00-EN.pdf.

Jabarin, Shawan. 2013. "The Occupied Palestinian Territory and international humanitarian law: a response to Peter Maurer." *International Review of the Red Cross* 95(890): 415–428.

Jamal, Amal. 2005. *The Palestinian National Movement: Politics of Contention: 1967–2005*. Bloomington: Indiana University Press.

Jovanovic, Zivadin. 2019. "Not to forget: 20 years since NATO aggression on Yugoslavia." – Interview by Enrico Vigna. *Belgrade Forum*, March 9, 2019. www.beoforum.rs/en/comments-belgrade-forum-for-the-world-of-equals/614-not-to-forget-20-years-since-nato-aggression-on-yugoslavia.html.

Khalidi, Rashid. 2006. *The Iron Cage: The Story of the Palestinian Struggle for Statehood*. Boston: Beacon Press.

Khouri, Rana B. 2011. "Western Sahara and Palestine: A Comparative Study of Colonialisms, Occupations, and Nationalisms." *New Middle Eastern Studies* 1: 1–20.

Koskenniemi, Martti. 1994. "National Self-determination Today: Problems of Legal Theory and Practice." *The International and Comparative Law Quarterly* 43(2): 241–269.

Laing, Edward. 1992. "The Norm of Self-Determination: 1941–1991." *California Western International Law Journal* 22: 209–308.

Masalha, Nur. 1992. *Expulsion of the Palestinians: The Concept of 'Transfer' in Zionist Political Thought 1882–1948*. Washington, D.C.: Institute for Palestine Studies.

Masalha, Nur. 2003. *The Politics of Denial: Israel and the Palestinian Refugee Problem*. London: Pluto Press.

Miguel, Carlos Ruiz. 2001. "Recientes Desarrollos del Conflicto del Sáhara Occidental: Autodeterminación y Estatalidad." *Anuario Mexicano de Derecho Internacional* 1, 343–362.

Momtaz, Djamchid. 2000. "NATO'S 'humanitarian intervention' in Kosovo and the prohibition of the use of force." *International Review of the Red Cross*, no. 837. www.icrc.org/en/doc/resources/documents/article/other/57jqcr.htm.

Morocco World News. 2018. "US Reaffirms that Morocco's Autonomy Plan is 'Serious, Credible and Realistic'." *Morocco World News*, 28 April 2018. www.moroccoworldnews.com/2018/04/245366/us-reaffirms-that-morocco-autonomy-plan-is-serious-credible-and-realistic/.

Ojeda-García, Raquel, Irene Fernández Molina, and Victoria Veguilla, eds. 2017. *Global, Regional and Local Dimensions of Western Sahara's Protracted Decolonization: When a Conflict Gets Old*. New York: Palgrave Macmillan.

Omar, Emboirik A. 2017. *El movimiento nacionalista saharaui: de Zemla a la Organización de la Unidad Africana*. Las Palmas: Mercurio.

Pappé, Ilan. 2006. "The 1948 Ethnic Cleansing of Palestine." *The Journal of Palestine Studies* 36(1): 6–20.

Por un Sahara Libre. 2018. "Victorias jurídicas sucesivas del Frente Polisario que sacuden el Reino de Marruecos." Accessed March 30, 2018. http://porunsaharalibre.org/2018/03/vitorias-juridicas-sucesivas-del-frente-polisario-que-sacuden-el-reino-de-marruecos/.

Rajagopal, Balakrishnan. 2003. "International Law and Social Movements: Challenges of Theorizing Resistance." *Columbia Journal of Transnational Law* 41(2): 397–433.

Roussellier, Jacques. 2014. "The Evolving Role of the United Nations: The Impossible Dual Track?" In *Perspectives on Western Sahara: Myths, Nationalisms and Geopolitics,* edited by Anouar Boukhars and Jacques Roussellier, 119–140. Lanham: Rowman and Littlefield.

Ruiz Miguel, Carlos. 2001. "Recientes Desarrollos del Conflicto del Sahara Occidental: Autodeterminación y Estatalidad." *Anuario Mexicano de Derecho Internacional* 1: 343–362.

Said, Edward. 2001. *The End of the Peace Process: Oslo and After.* New York: Vintage Books.

Said, Edward. 2003. *The Question of Palestine.* New York: Vintage Books.

Saleh, Mohsen. 2014. *The Palestinian Issue: Historical Background and Contemporary Developments.* Beirut: Al-Zaytouna Centre for Studies and Consultations.

Sahara Rise. 2018. "Sahara Rise Manifest." Accessed July 20, 2019. http://sahararise.org/en/sahara-rise-manifest/.

Shlaim, Avi. 2005. "The Rise and Fall of the Oslo Peace Process." In *International Relations of the Middle East,* edited by Louise Fawcett, 241–261. Oxford: Oxford University Press.

Soares, Adérito de Jesus. 2012. "The Parallels and the Paradox of Timor-Leste and Western Sahara." In *Autonomy and Separatism in South and Southeast Asia,* edited by Michelle Miller, 77–92. Singapore: Institute of Southeast Asia Studies.

Tilley, Virginia. 2012. *Beyond Occupation: Apartheid, Colonialism and International Law in the Occupied Palestinian Territories.* London: Pluto Press.

Turner, Mandy. 2015. "Peacebuilding as counterinsurgency in the occupied Palestinian territories." *Review of International Studies* 41: 73–98.

United Nations. 1942. "Declaration of the United Nations." Accessed November 2, 2019.
www.un.org/en/sections/history-united-nations-charter/1942-declaration-united-nations/index.html.

United Nations General Assembly. 2017. *Report on the Right of peoples to self-determination: report of the Secretary General*, A/72/317 (11 August 2017), available from undocs.org/pdf?symbol=en/A/72/317.

United Nations Office of the High Commissioner for Human Rights. 2014. *Report of the Independent Expert on the promotion of a democratic and equitable international order exploring the adverse impacts of military expenditures on the realization of a democratic and equitable international order*, A/HRC/27/51 (17 July 2014), available from http://ap.ohchr.org/documents/dpage_e.aspx?si=A/HRC/27/51.

United Nations General Assembly. 1947. *Future government of Palestine*, A/RES/181(II) (29 November 1947), available from unispal.un.org/DPA/DPR/unispal.nsf/0/7F0AF2BD897689B785256C330061D253.

United Nations General Assembly. 1948. *Palestine – Progress Report of the*

United Nations Mediator, A/RES/194(III) (11 December 1948), available from unispal.un.org/DPA/DPR/unispal.nsf/0/C758572B78D1CD0085256BCF0077E51A.

United Nations General Assembly. 1960. *Declaration on the granting of independence to colonial countries and peoples*, A/RES/1514(XV) (14 December 1960).

United Nations General Assembly. 1965. *Question of Ifni and Spanish Sahara*, A/RES/2072(XX) (16 December 1965), available from undocs.org/en/A/RES/2072(XX).

United Nations General Assembly. 1966. *International Covenant on Civil and Political Rights,* A/RES/2200A(XXI) (16 December 1966), available from www.un.org/en/development/desa/population/migration/generalassembly/docs/globalcompact/A_RES_2200A(XXI)_civil.pdf.

United Nations General Assembly. 1966. *International Covenant on Economic, Social and Cultural Rights*, A/RES/2200A(XXI) (16 December 1966), available from www.un.org/en/development/desa/population/migration/generalassembly/docs/globalcompact/A_RES_2200A(XXI)_economic.pdf.

United Nations General Assembly. 1974. *Question of Spanish Sahara*, A/RES/3292(XXIX) (13 December 1974), available from digitallibrary.un.org/record/190206/files/A_RES_3292%28XXIX%29-EN.pdf.

United Nations General Assembly. 1974. *Question of Palestine*, A/RES/3236 (XXIX) (22 November 1974), available from undocs.org/A/RES/3236%20(XXIX).

United Nations General Assembly. 1975. *Invitation to the Palestine Liberation Organization to participate in the efforts for peace in the Middle East*, A/RES/3375(XXX) (10 November 1975).

United Nations General Assembly. 1975. *Question of Palestine*, A/RES/3376(XXX) (10 November 1975).

United Nations General Assembly. 2005. *Respect for the principles of national sovereignty and diversity of democratic systems in electoral processes as an important element for the promotion and protection of human rights*, A/RES/60/164 (16 December 2005).

United Nations General Assembly. 2017. *Universal realization of the right of peoples to self-determination*, A/RES/72/159 (19 December 2017).

United Nations. 2017. *Special Committee on Decolonization Adopts 2 Information-Related Draft Resolutions as It Opens 2017 Substantive Session*. GA/COL/3311, 12 June 2017.

UNRWA. 2019. "UNRWA in Figures 2018." Accessed September 10, 2019. https://www.unrwa.org/resources/about-unrwa/unrwa-figures-2018.

Veracini, Lorenzo. 2010. *Settler Colonialism: A Theoretical Overview*. London: Palgrave Macmillan.

White House. 2015. "5 Things You Need to Know About the US-Israel Relationship Under President Obama." Accessed July 20, 2019. www.whitehouse.gov/blog/2015/03/01/5-things-you-need-know-about-us-israel-relationship-under-president-obama.

Wolfe, Patrick. 1999. *Settler Colonialism and the Transformation of Anthropology: The Politics and Poetics of an Ethnographic Event*. London: Cassell.

Zartman, I. William. 2014. "Morrocco's Saharan Policy." In *Perspectives on Western Sahara: Myths, Nationalisms and Geopolitics*, edited by Anouar Boukhars and Jacques Roussellier, 55–70. Lanham: Rowman and Littlefield.

Zoubir, Yahia H. 2007. "Stalemate in Western Sahara: Ending International Legality." *Middle East Policy* 14(4): 158–177.

Zunes, Stephen, and Jacob Mundy. 2010. *Western Sahara: War, Nationalism, and Conflict Irresolution.* New York: Syracuse University Press.

Zunes, Stephen, and Jacob Mundy. 2015. "Moroccan Settlers in Western Sahara: Colonists or Fifth Column?" In *Settlers in Contested Lands: Territorial Disputes and Ethnic Conflicts*, edited by Oded Haklai and Neophytus Loizides, 40–74. Stanford: Stanford University Press.

8

Self-Determination and State Sovereignty: The Case of UN Involvement in Jammu and Kashmir

STEPHEN P. WESTCOTT

The year 2018 marks the 70th anniversary of the First Indo-Pakistani War over Jammu and Kashmir (simplified as Kashmir from hereon in) and United Nations (UN) Security Council Resolution 47. This resolution stipulated that both India and Pakistan should withdraw their military forces and arrange for a plebiscite to be held in order to provide the people of Kashmir the choice of which state to join (S/RES/47). Ostensibly this resolution was an effort by the UN Security Council to put the right to self-determination into practice. Yet I argue that a closer inspection reveals that the Security Council, by limiting the choice for the people of Kashmir to accession into either India or Pakistan, and its lackadaisical efforts to implement the plebiscite the resolution called for, was in fact privileging another norm: the existing sovereign state's rights. The basis for this decision is at the heart of the UN Charter itself. Although the UN Charter famously calls for the 'equal rights and self-determination of peoples' in Article 1, Article 2 also clearly states 'nothing contained in the present [UN] Charter shall authorise the UN to intervene in matters that are essentially within the jurisdiction of any state' (1945, 3). As the peoples seeking self-determination are inherently within a state, the norm of self-determination typically finds itself in conflict with the norm of state territorial integrity. The situation becomes further confused when the people in question occupy a territory that is contested between two sovereign states, as is the case in Kashmir.

The Kashmir situation is far from unique. Though few other self-determination movements exist within territory actively disputed between two states, the UN has been consistently reluctant to recognise any self-determination movements seeking to break from already recognised states. This remains the case whether the movements have already established a *de facto* state, such as Somaliland and Transnistria, or are aspirant independence movements, such as those undertaken by the Tibetans, Kurds or West Papuans. This chapter is dedicated to illuminating the tension that exists between the principle of self-determination and the rights of state sovereignty that is inherent within the UN. In using the case of Jammu and Kashmir, one of the earliest incidences where this normative clash occurred, this chapter demonstrates that while the UN formerly advocates for self-determination, it in practice upholds the principle of territorial sovereignty. However, before we can explore the history and ramifications of the UN Security Council's actions concerning Kashmir, we must first define these terms, explore why they are often in conflict with each other and how the UN has sought to employ them.

Self-Determination, Sovereign Territorial Integrity and the UN

One significant source of tension that exists within the theory and practice of international law is between the principle of self-determination and the norm of state sovereignty, especially when it concerns the state's territorial integrity. Broadly defined, self-determination is the philosophical and political principle that people should have the right to shape their own political, economic and/or cultural destiny. In contrast, the norm of sovereignty refers to the claim of a state, recognised by other states, to be the exclusive political authority within a specific territory. Whilst self-determination is often the foundation for a state, it becomes an issue when an aspirant people seek to separate from an established state, either attempting to establish their own separate state (secessionism) or to join another state (irredentism) (Taras and Ganguly 2006, 41–44). The norm of state sovereignty has two primary components.

The first is the principle of non-interference, or the expectation that states should be free to conduct their internal affairs without any outside interference. The second is the principle of territorial integrity, or that a state's borders are sacrosanct and thereby should not be altered without the consent of all relevant parties. In other words, the territorial integrity aspect of the norm does not recognise the right of people to engage in a unilateral secession, whilst the non-interference requirement ensures that international actors cannot legitimately compel the state to do so (Makinda 1998, 103–105). Hence, the principle of self-determination frequently finds itself in conflict with the norm of state sovereignty.

Interestingly, despite the UN's well-earned reputation for being divided and equivocating upon many issues, it has been surprisingly united and consistent in its favouring the norms of non-interference and the territorial integrity of a sovereign state over the self-determination of peoples. The only example of the UN unequivocally embracing the principle of self-determination was its support movement for decolonisation. This consideration was most clearly articulated in two General Assembly's declarations. The first of these was Resolution 1514(XV), more commonly known as the Declaration Granting Independence to Colonial Territories, Countries and Peoples, proclaimed in December 1960. This declaration decreed that 'the subjection of peoples to alien subjugation, domination and exploitation… is contrary to the Charter of the United Nations' and proclaimed that 'all peoples have the right to self-determination; by virtue of this right they freely determine their political status and to pursue their economic, social and cultural development' (A/RES/1514[XV]).

The second declaration was Resolution 2625(XXV), more commonly known as the Declaration on Principles of International Law, Friendly Relations and Co-operation Among States in accordance with the Charter of the United Nations, proclaimed in October 1970. This declaration explicitly stated that the principle of self-determination's goal was 'to bring a speedy end to colonialism, having due regard for the freely expressed will of the peoples concerned' (A/RES/2625[XXV]). Furthermore, it specified that 'the estalishment of a sovereign or independent state, the free association or integration with an independent State or the emergence into any other political status freely determined by a people constitute modes of implementing the right of self-determination' (ibid.).

However, once the process of decolonisation is complete, the focus of the right to self-determination within the UN organs shifts from the people to the state itself. Indeed, the Declaration on Principles of International Law proclaimed:

> Nothing in the forgoing paragraphs shall be construed as authorising or encouraging any action which would dismember or impair, totally or in part, the territorial integrity or political unity of sovereign and independent states conducting themselves in compliance with the principle of equal rights and self-determination of peoples described above and thus possessed of a government representing the whole people belonging to the territory without distinction as to race, creed or colour (ibid.).

In other words, the General Assembly was asserting that once the process of decolonisation is complete, the state's sovereign rights to territorial integrity and political autonomy take precedence. The basis of this post-colonial pivot towards the norm of state sovereignty is based upon the principle of *uti possidetis*. In essence, the principle of *uti possidetis* stipulates that when a former colony secedes from an empire, the new state's borders should match its former administrative boundaries (Taras and Ganguly 2006, 45). Any alteration of these borders only occurring after an international agreement involving the new state or with the state's own consent. Thus, any unilateral efforts by secessionist or irredentist movements to break away from an existing state are not recognised by any UN organs, with such actions only becoming legitimate if the existing state accepts the split (Chandhoke 2008, 2–4).

In part, the adoption of the principle of *uti possidetis* has been purely pragmatic owing to the difficulty of adequately establishing a territorial state that does not contain some minority within it and the general reluctance for established states to accept being bifurcated. Yet the favouring of the nation-state has also been partly adopted by design, with several scholars arguing that an unstated goal of the UN has been to freeze the political and territorial map after the process of de-colonisation (Saini 2001, 60–65; Taras and Ganguly 2006, 45–46).

By and large, this freezing of territorial boundaries has been a boon for international peace as the late twentieth century saw a marked reduction of interstate wars over territory and for 'national reunification'. Indeed, most of the international community could agree that the maintenance of colonies was against the principle of self-determination and that as colonies are by definition not part of a state's core territory, they were hard to justify by appealing to their sovereignty. However, this peace has come at the UN's sacrifice of a broader application of the principle of self-determination to any aspirant non-self-governing peoples in non-colonial states who see little future within their current borders or otherwise wish to break away. During the UN's first five years, there were several cases of non-self-governing territories that the General Assembly or Security Council could have sought to apply the principle of self-determination to any aspirant peoples rather than defer to existing state interests.[1] One of the most prominent of these cases was the India-Pakistan conflict over Kashmir.

The Origins of the Jammu and Kashmir Dispute

---

[1] Apart for the situation in Kashmir, two of the most notable examples from this period are the UN General Assembly's 1947 vote to accept the partitioning of Palestine (A/RES/181B[II]) and 1950 vote to accept the federation of Ethiopia and Eritrea (A/REES/390A[V]), over the objections of the Arab and Eritrean populations respectively.

During British rule, the subcontinent was governed in part through territories that British authorities directly administered and in part through a number of semi-autonomous vassals known as Princely States. One of the largest of these Princely States was Jammu and Kashmir, situated in the northwest corner of British India. The territory came under British suzerainty in 1846 when the British East India Company sold the Valley of Kashmir to the Raja of Jammu, Gulab Singh, and recognised him as a Maharaja in return for his acceptance of British overlordship (Schofield 2000, 7–10). When the British withdrew from the subcontinent in 1947, they partitioned their former colony roughly along sectarian lines to create India and Pakistan in a futile effort to reduce the bloodshed between supporters of the bitterly feuding All India National Congress of Mahatma Gandhi and Jawaharlal Nehru and the Muslim League of Muhammad Ali Jinnah. As part of this partition, all the Princely States would be forced to sign the Instruments of Accession which would incorporate their lands into one of the new states. Although the respective 'princes' could choose which state their realm would be absorbed into, they were encouraged by the British to consider both their geographical location and the demographics of their subjects (Behera 2006, 5–14).

At the time of the British withdrawal, Kashmir was approximately 77% Muslim and bordering the western wing of Pakistan. This would have theoretically ensured that joining Pakistan would have been a natural choice. However, there also existed several minorities within Kashmir which favoured India, most notably the Buddhist Ladakhis in the north and the Sikhs and Hindu Dogras in the south (Behera 2006, 104–105). Additionally, the Muslim population of Kashmir was not homogeneous, with many following the mystic Sufi tradition of Islam with significant pockets of Shia and orthodox Sunni populations (Snedden 2013, 9–10). A final issue came from the political leanings of the local authorities and personalities of Kashmir. Although there were supporters for acceding to either India and Pakistan, the key Kashmiri political actors at the time were the Hindu Maharajah, Hari Singh, and the leader of the All Jammu and Kashmir National Conference, Sheikh Abdullah.

Singh had ruled Kashmir with increasing despotism since he ascended to the throne in 1925, paying little attention to his ministers or local council when passing laws, imposing discriminatory taxes on Muslims. As a result, Singh was a highly unpopular ruler and often had to use his military, often with the assistance of British forces, to crush local unrest (Schofield 2000, 17–18). Nonetheless, as the Maharajah, Singh was empowered to make the decision whether to accede his kingdom to India or Pakistan. However, Singh personally disliked both Jinnah and Nehru and clearly wished to maintain his control over Kashmir. Thus, Singh deliberately equivocated in declaring for either India or Pakistan, seemingly believing that by delaying the decision he could achieve *de facto* independence for Kashmir (Subbiah 2004, 175).

Abdullah and the All Jammu and Kashmir National Conference represented the main local opposition to Singh. Hence, their primary policy aims were concerned with ending the Maharaja's rule and establishing a secular representative government in Kashmir. Yet, while Abdullah hated the ideological concept of Pakistan and was good friends with Nehru, his clearly preferred status for Kashmir since 1944 was to establish it as 'an independent political unit like Switzerland in South Asia' (Lamb 1991, 187–190; Snedden 2013, 25).

By the end of October 1947, two months after Britain formally withdrew from the subcontinent, both India and Pakistan were growing impatient for Singh to make his accession decision. It was Pakistan, increasingly convinced that India was trying to smother it or at least cheat it out of economic and strategically important territory, that moved first (Hajari 2015, 180–189). In an effort to secure Kashmir for Pakistan, several members of the Pakistani military and government orchestrated an invasion of pro-Pakistan Islamic zealots from the Pashtun tribes on Pakistan's western frontier. The Maharaja's forces, already occupied trying to pacify an unrelated anti-Maharaja pro-Pakistan rebellion in the Poonch region, were completely unprepared to resist such an invasion and were swiftly routed. India refused to assist unless Singh signed the Instrument of Accession in favour of India. Thus Singh, recognising that his political position had collapsed and desperate to gain Indian help in repulsing the invasion, formally signed the document in favour of India on 26 October 1947 (Schofield 2000, 41–54).

Despite the obviously coerced nature of Singh's signature and the fact that it went against the pro-Pakistan or independence aspirations of many Kashmiris, India's leadership was convinced that Singh's accession gave India both the legal and moral right to the Princely State. This mentality was buttressed by the fact that India was able to rush in enough troops to halt the advance of Pakistan's proxy forces upon the Kashmiri capital of Srinagar and even reverse some of their territorial gains. However, India was not able to inject enough troops into Kashmir to advance far before winter made further operations impossible. With the weather ending any further campaigning from either side, Nehru decided to call upon the Security Council to mediate believing the UN would compel Pakistan to withdraw (Subbiah 2004, 176–177). Thus, on 1 January 1948, Nehru wrote a letter to the UN Security Council (S/628), arguing that:

> Under Article 35 of the Charter of the United Nations, any member may bring any situation, whose continuance is likely to endanger the maintenance of international peace and security to the attention of the Security Council. Such a

situation now exists between India and Pakistan owing to the aid which invaders...are drawing from Pakistan for operations against Jammu and Kashmir, a State which acceded to the Dominion of India...The Government of India requests the Security Council to call upon Pakistan to put to an end immediately...[this] act of aggression against India.[2]

Pakistan responded with their own letter to the UN Security Council on 15 January 1948 (S/646), rejecting India's claims, outlining its own position concerning Kashmir and airing several other grievances regarding India's conduct.

Much to India's indignation, the UN Security Council did not order Pakistan to withdraw but instead passed Resolution 39 on 20 January 1948 establishing the UN Commission for India and Pakistan (UNCIP). The UNCIP was empowered to investigate the facts on the ground and act as a mediator between India and Pakistan and to resolve the dispute (S/RES/39). Notwithstanding the Security Council's efforts, combat operations began to resume in February, with both sides clashing as soon as the territory began to thaw. After a few months of deliberation, the UN Security Council passed the more detailed Resolution 47 on 21 April 1948 in an effort to provide the basic guidelines for resolving the conflict. In essence, Resolution 47 called upon Pakistan to secure the withdrawal of its proxies, followed by a withdrawal of Indian troops. The UN would then establish a temporary Plebiscite Administration in Kashmir, with the mandate to conduct a fair and impartial plebiscite 'on the question of the accession of the State to India or Pakistan' (S/RES/47). To oversee the implementation of this Resolution, the UNCIP was expanded and immediately dispatched to the subcontinent.

UN Involvement in the Jammu and Kashmir Dispute

The clear intention of Resolution 47 was to put into practice the principle of self-determination. However, in practice the question of self-determination was quickly superseded by concerns about international peace. Indeed, by the time the UNCIP arrived in July, on the 20 April 1948 Jinnah which authorised the Pakistan Army to occupy the territory held by their tribal proxies and pro-Pakistani rebels, had begun to be pushed back by an Indian offensive. Although this order was given prior to Resolution 47, Pakistan disregarded the UN Resolution's call for a ceasefire and withdrawal, with

---

[2] The Article 35 referred to in India's letter is part of Chapter VI of the UN Charter which stipulates that the Security Council has the right to investigate any international dispute or situation likely to endanger international peace (Article 34) and recommends appropriate procedures or terms to resolve the dispute (Articles 36, 37 and 38).

Pakistani Army units arriving in force in May. Hence, the UNCIP considered its duty first and foremost to be brokering a truce between India and Pakistan rather than any efforts to determine the Kashmiris' desires or even lay the groundwork for a plebiscite. To that end, the Commission passed a resolution on 13 August 1948 proposing that both sides issue a ceasefire and accept a truce overseen by the UN (S/1100, 28–30). However, this plan was largely unimaginative, with the UNCIP simply proposing that the ceasefire be monitored by UN observers before reiterating the model for resolving the dispute outlined in Resolution 47.

Although both India and Pakistan eventually agreed to a ceasefire and a Line of Control, which came into effect on 1 January 1949, the UNCIP was unable to broker any agreement as to how to demilitarise Kashmir or how the plebiscite should be conducted (Snedden 2005, 72–74). Pakistan remained unwilling to withdraw its forces, believing that India had attempted to seize Kashmir using 'fraud and violence' and would not uphold its obligations (Subbiah 2004, 178–179). Pakistan therefore insisted upon more details as to how the plebiscite would be held and for any Pakistani withdrawal to be synchronised with India's military (see Annex 1 in S/1196, 12–14). India for its part took the position that the Instrument of Accession made Kashmir legitimately part of India and that Pakistan had launched an unprovoked war of aggression to annex the territory. Hence, India considered that it was the UNCIP's role to force Pakistan to withdraw, refusing to move before Pakistan and remaining lukewarm on the necessity of holding a plebiscite (Hajari 2015, 246).

Although the UNCIP's focus had quickly turned to ending the war between India and Pakistan, it did at least attempt to uphold the principle of self-determination by continuing to insist on holding a plebiscite. However, the history of multiple UN efforts to implement the plebiscite in Kashmir illustrates how it was already beginning to defer to the norm of state sovereignty whenever it clashed with the principle of self-determination. This policy approach manifested in two significant ways. Firstly, the UNCIP and its successors largely neglected to consult or otherwise engage with the various political actors within Kashmir itself. It is recorded that some UNCIP members did stay in Srinagar from 1 to 9 September 1948, during which time they met with Sheik Abdullah at least once (S/1100, 75). However, there is no mention or elaboration of what was discussed or observed. The Commission also reported receiving several letters and having an 'informal' meeting with the pro-Pakistan 'Azad Kashmir Government' (S/1100, 15 and 41).

Regardless, it is evident that the Commission paid little heed to these Kashmiri authorities, disregarding their calls to place greater emphasis on the plebiscite and recognising them only as 'local authorities' (Snedden 2013, 88–89). Although the UNCIP formally recognised Sheik Abdullah as the 'Prime Minister of the State of Jammu and Kashmir', it mostly avoided engaging with him and his administration throughout their time on the subcontinent. The UNCIP also went to great lengths to avoid indirectly bestowing any legitimacy upon the Azad Kashmir officials, explicitly resolving to 'avoid an action which might be interpreted as signifying *de facto* or *de jure* recognition of the "Azad Kashmir Government"' (S/1100, 25). There is no evidence that the UNCIP attempted to meet, interview or correspond with Maharaja Hari Singh. These decisions by the UNCIP to disregard these 'local authorities' clearly stemmed from its belief that its mandate was to mediate between the governments in New Delhi and Karachi rather than identifying the preferences of Kashmiris. Hence, in choosing to recognise India and Pakistan as the only parties to the dispute, UNCIP was deferring to the norm of state sovereignty rather than engage in a genuine effort to advance the principle of self-determination.

Secondly, the UNCIP and the Security Council clearly considered the Kashmir conflict to be simply a territorial dispute between India and Pakistan. Hence, at no point does the Security Council or its agents appear to have countenanced any option of independence for Kashmir. Indeed, there is no mention in any of the UNCIP's three reports (S/1100, S/1196 and S/1430) of even a discussion over whether the proposed plebiscite should include an option other than a straightforward vote as to which state to join. Yet this is in stark contrast to the wishes of the dominant political force in Kashmir during this period, Sheik Abdullah. Although Abdullah clearly favoured India over Pakistan, he seemingly preferred to achieve Kashmiri independence or, failing that, ensure that Kashmir effectively remains a semi-autonomous protectorate rather than a regular state of India (Lamb 1991, 191–195). Indeed, during this period, Abdullah frequently argued, to any foreign dignitary that would listen, the necessity of including the option for independence on any plebiscite so that the people of Kashmir could determine where their 'true well-being lies' (Lamb 1991, 189–190; Snedden 2005, 83). It is unclear what support the option for independence had amongst the majority of Kashmiris.

Nonetheless, the point still stands that having the option in a plebiscite would have more holistically encompassed their right to determine their political destiny that is at the heart of the principle of self-determination. In disregarding such sentiments, the UNCIP and the Security Council were, intentionally or not, accepting that India and Pakistan were the sole successor states of British India and thereby tacitly implementing the principle of *uti possidetis* even at this early stage.

In December 1949, the UNCIP submitted its final report to the Security

Council in which it frankly acknowledged its failure to mediate the dispute between India and Pakistan or convince them to demilitarise. Although, the UNCIP maintained that a plebiscite remained the most effective means of determining legitimate sovereignty over Kashmir, it did state that the framework established in Resolution 47 was already 'a rather outmoded pattern' and suggested that their successors should consider alternative methods of resolution, including arbitration (S/1430, 78–79). Hence, the Security Council decided to appoint what turned out to be a series of individual representatives empowered with greater flexibility to mediate between India and Pakistan and try to pave the way for the plebiscite.

Arguably the most notable of these was the Australian judge and diplomat, Sir Owen Dixon. Although Dixon, like all the Security Council's delegations, dealt primarily with the governments of India and Pakistan, he was unique in that he based himself in Srinagar for a full month between June and July 1950. Interestingly, Dixon notes that he had 'more than one interview with Sheik Abdullah' but, like the UNCIP, he did not elaborate as to what was discussed during them (S/1791, 3). During his stay in Kashmir, Dixon travelled extensively throughout the disputed territory and therefore recognised more clearly than other UN officials that the straightforward plebiscite outlined in Resolution 47 was unworkable. Indeed, he noted in his report that 'the State of Jammu and Kashmir is not really a unit geographically, demographically or economically. It is an agglomeration of territories brought under the power of one Maharajah' (S/1791, 28). Indeed, it was evident that the Buddhist Ladakhi and the Hindu Dogra minorities feared being oppressed by a Muslim Kashmiri majority, whether this was in Pakistan or as part of an independent Kashmir (Behera 2006, 109–114).

In response to this issue, and the seeming inability of India and Pakistan to agree on virtually anything, Dixon proposed that the plan for the plebiscite outlined in Resolution 47 be modified in order to resolve the Kashmir dispute. Specifically, Dixon argued that the situation within Kashmir ultimately required that it be partitioned and suggested two potential models for how to do so. The first proposed breaking the former Princely State into different ethnonationalist regions which would vote as to which country they would prefer. The second model proposed simply allocating those areas that were certain to prefer accession to either India or Pakistan respectively and then holding a plebiscite in the uncertain territory of the Valley of Kashmir itself (S/1791, 17–18). Though the Indian government initially indicated it was willing to explore a division of Kashmir, Pakistan refused to divert from the original plebiscite plan ensuring that Dixon's suggestions were ultimately rejected by both states. The UN Security Council also proved unwilling to force the issue and simply continued to exhort the two feuding states to continue negotiations (Snedden 2005, 75).

After Dixon, the UN Security Council appointed two further representatives to ensure the ceasefire held, and tried to induce India and Pakistan to demilitarise Kashmir so the plebiscite could be held or to find some other way around the impasse. However, neither seriously engaged the local Kashmiri authorities, and instead fruitlessly attempted to coax the increasingly disinterested and sceptical India and Pakistan into some form of agreement (Lamb 1991, 175–178). India's willingness to hold the plebiscite quickly waned as it began to realise that it was unlikely to win any popular vote regarding Kashmir's accession. Furthermore, India grew increasingly truculent and obstructionist towards any UN proposals, believing that the Security Council generally, and Britain and the US especially, were biased towards Pakistan (Ankit 2010; Hingorani 2016, 192–217). Though Pakistan was ostensibly more amenable to holding a plebiscite, it remained distrustful of India and refused to make any first move. The prospects of holding a successful plebiscite were further spoiled by the frequent and ruthless suppression of Kashmiri rights on both sides of the Line of Control soon after the 1949 ceasefire. India organised the dismissal and arrest of Sheik Abdullah in 1953 for his pro-independence stance, replacing him with a series of pro-Indian puppets who were kept in office via allegedly rigged elections (Lamb 1991, 199–204; Snedden 2005, 75). Pakistan similarly began administering the areas of Kashmir it controlled autocratically, establishing a puppet government in Azad Kashmir and governing the northern areas of Gilgit and Baltistan directly.

In late-1954, Nehru unilaterally declared that the US's alliance with Pakistan had 'changed the whole context of the Kashmir issue' and that the plebiscite was no longer an option that India supported (Snedden 2005, 75–76). The UN Security Council eventually responded by passing Resolution 122 in January 1957, which expressed the UN's frustration with the lack of progress and restated its position that the future of Kashmir could only be decided by a free and fair plebiscite (S/RES/122). However, the UN remained unwilling to force the issue by imposing sanctions or other measures that would undermine state sovereignty. Gradually the UN gave up trying to enact the principle of self-determination for Kashmir. In 1958, the UN neglected to appoint another representative for India and Pakistan, effectively washing its hands of the issue. Indeed, during both the 1965 and 1971 India-Pakistan wars, the Security Council only passed resolutions demanding a ceasefire between the two sides, making no reference to the people of Kashmir or the right to self-determination (see S/RES/211 and S/RES/307).

The UN, Self-Determination and Jammu and Kashmir Today

As the Kashmir case demonstrates, the UN's deference to state sovereignty over the principle of self-determination was demonstrated early in its history. Whilst there was the possibility for the UN to have strengthened the principle of self-determination during its earlier years, that moment has well and truly passed. By the 1970s, the debates within the UN General Assembly and Security Council established the principle that only colonised peoples had an explicit right to self-determination. This position has led supporters of India's position, especially to point out that Kashmir is not a colony and therefore the arguments for Kashmiri self-determination do not apply (Hingorani 2016, 166–171; Saini 2001, 72–73). Although the UN Security Council has largely accepted this logic and disengaged from the Kashmir conflict, it does continue to maintain a formal interest in the form of the UN Military Observer Group in India and Pakistan, which continues to monitor activities on both sides of the Line of Control.

In recent years, the focus of the UN has again turned to Kashmir, albeit due to the human right concerns rather than engaging in any effort to uphold the principle of self-determination. Since 1989, a medium-intensity insurgency has raged in Indian Administered Kashmir, triggered in large part by desires for greater self-determination and Kashmiri frustration over India's erosion of local autonomy. Although the Kashmir insurgency was originally driven by secessionist sentiments, it was quickly hijacked by Islamist insurgents several of whom were supported by Pakistan. India's response has been draconian only serving to alienate much of the Kashmiri population (Mohan et al. 2019). A new wave of unrest erupted in 2016 after Indian security forces killed Burhan Wani, a young and popular local insurgent commander, and the Indian Army and paramilitary police responded with crackdowns. This prompted the first significant UN action on Kashmir in decades, with the UN Human Rights Commission (UNHRC) publishing a report identifying numerous human rights abuses committed by the Indian Army during its efforts to crush the unrest (OHCHR 2018). While the UNHRC report also addressed similar issues in Pakistan Administer Kashmir, India strongly rejected the findings of the report, declaring it to be fallacious, prejudiced and a violation of its 'sovereignty and territorial integrity' (MEA 2018). In response, the UNHRC simply stated it was 'disappointed' with India's reaction to the report, with the General Assembly and Security Council taking no action or making any comment (Mohan 2018).

On 5 August 2019, the last vestiges of Kashmiri self-determination in India were removed when the recently re-elected Bharatiya Janata Party government placed Kashmiri political leaders under house arrest, revoked the articles in the Indian Constitution which made Kashmir an autonomous Indian state and broke Ladakh off to be an independent province. Although Kashmiri self-determination has been eroded by Indian centralisation efforts in the past, this move makes Kashmir a Union Territory that will be directly administrated from New Delhi, albeit with its own legislature to handle local issues (BBC 2019; Rej 2019). Pakistan vehemently condemned India's move, pledging to raise the issue at the UN Security Council and potentially take it to the International Court of Justice (Hashim 2019). Pakistan eventually convinced its tacit ally China to call for an emergency closed door session of the Security Council on 16 August 2019, marking the first time in decades that the UN body had directly considered the Kashmir issue. However, the Council ultimately took no action, and instead urged both sides to 'refrain from taking any unilateral action which might further aggravate the...situation' (UN News 2019). The UN Secretary-General, Antonio Guterres, also released a statement appealing for 'maximum restraint' and reiterating the UN's position that 'the status of Jammu and Kashmir is to be settled by peaceful means, in accordance with the UN Charter' (UN News 2019).

These exchanges are characteristic of the UN's conduct towards issues of self-determination more generally; the UN's inherent preference over upholding state sovereign rights ensures that it remains reluctant to act or even pressure an existing sovereign state over issues of self-determination. Generally speaking, this stance by the UN has helped maintain international peace by establishing the state's post-colonial borders as a clear and workable template for resolving interstate disputes. However, the UN's commitment to non-interference and the principle of *uti possidetis* also means that the UN remains far from being a friend of self-determination as such. Rather, the UN's position often ensures that any aspirant self-determination movement's demands need to be accepted by existing sovereign state(s) before the international community can even formally engage with them. Thus, most contemporary self-determination movements frequently develop an antagonistic, if not outright combative, relationship with the state(s) they reside in, as the case of Kashmir also ultimately demonstrates. Without some dramatic change of heart from India, Pakistan or the UN Security Council, the people of Kashmir are unlikely to see an end to the stalemate or any genuine chance to choose their destiny anytime soon.

References

Ankit, Rakesh. 2010. "1948: The Crucial Year in the History of Jammu and Kashmir." *Economic and Political Weekly* 45 (13): 49–58.

BBC. 2019. "Article 370: India strips disputed Kashmir of special status." *BBC*, August 5, 2019. https://www.bbc.com/news/world-asia-india-49231619.

Behera, Navnita Chadha. 2006. *Demystifying Kashmir*. Washington D.C.: Brookings Institution Press.

Chandhoke, Neera. 2008. "Exploring the Right to Secession: The South Asian Context." *South Asia Research* 28 (1): 1–22.

Hajari, Nisid. 2015. *Midnight's Furies: The Deadly Legacy of India's Partition*. Stroud: Amberly Publishing.

Hashim, Asad. 2019. "Pakistan's Khan Calls for International Intervention in Kashmir" *Al Jazeera*, August 6, 2019.
https://www.aljazeera.com/news/southasia/2019/08/pakistan-khan-calls-international-intervention-kashmir-190806131911914.html.

Hingorani, Aman M. 2016. *Unravelling the Kashmir Knot*. New Delhi: SAGE Publications India.

Lamb, Alastair. 1991. *Kashmir: A Disputed Legacy, 1846–1990*. Hertingfordbury: Roxford Books.

Makinda, Samuel. 1998. "The United Nations and State Sovereignty: Mechanism for Managing International Security." *Australian Journal of Political Science* 33 (1): 101–115.

Ministry of External Affairs (MEA), Government of India. 2018. "Official Spokesperson's response to a question on the Report by the Office of the High Commissioner for Human Rights on 'The human rights situation in Kashmir'." June 14, 2018. https://bit.ly/2sjUoFe.

Mohan, Dinesh, Harsh Mander, Navsharan Singh, Pamela Philipose, and Tapan Bose. 2019. *Dateline Kashmir: Inside the Worlds most Militarised Zone*. Clayton: Monash University Press.

Mohan, Geeta. 2018. "India's reaction to Kashmir report disappointing, says human rights body." *India Today*, July 18, 2018.
https://www.indiatoday.in/india/story/indian-reaction-to-kashmir-report-disappointing-says-human-rights-body-1289709-2018-07-18.

OHCHR. 2018. *Report on the Situation of Human Rights in Kashmir: Developments in the Indian State of Jammu and Kashmir from June 2016 to April 2018, and General Human Rights Concerns in Azad Jammu and Kashmir and Gilgit-Baltistan*. UN: Office of the High Commissioner for Human Rights. https://www.ohchr.org/Documents/Countries/IN/DevelopmentsInKashmirJune2016ToApril2018.pdf.

Rej, Abhijnan. 2019. "Modi-fying Kashmir: Unpacking India's Historic Decision to Revoke Kashmir's Autonomy" *The Diplomat*, August 6, 2019. https://thediplomat.com/2019/08/modi-fying-kashmir-unpacking-indias-historic-decision-to-revoke-kashmirs-autonomy/.

Saini, R.S. 2001. "Self-determination, Terrorism and Kashmir." *India Quarterly* 57 (2): 59–98.

Schofield, Victoria. 2000. *Kashmir in Conflict: India, Pakistan and the Unending War*. London: I.B. Tauris.

Snedden, Christopher. 2005. "Would a plebiscite have resolved the Kashmir Dispute?" *South Asia: Journal of South Asian Studies*, 28 (1): 64–88.

Snedden, Christopher. 2013. *Kashmir: The Unwritten History*. Noida UP: Harper Collins Publishers India.

Subbiah, Sumathi. 2004. "Security Council Mediation and the Kashmir Dispute: Reflections on its Failures and Possibilities for Renewal." *Boston College International and Comparative Law Review* 27 (1): 173–185.

Taras, Raymond C. and Rajat Ganguly. 2006. *Understanding Ethnic Conflict*. 4th ed. Abington: Routledge.

UN News. 2019. "UN Security Council discusses Kashmir, China urges India and Pakistan to ease tensions." *UN News*, August 16, 2019. https://news.un.org/en/story/2019/08/1044401.

UNCIP, *United Nations Commission in India and Pakistan Interim Report*, S/1100 (9 November 1948), available from https://undocs.org/S/1100.

UNCIP, *United Nations Commission in India and Pakistan Second Interim Report*, S/1196 (10 January 1949), available from https://undocs.org/S/1196.

UNCIP, *United Nations Commission in India and Pakistan Third Interim Report*, S/1430 (9 December 1949), available from https://undocs.org/S/1430.

United Nations. 1945. *Charter of the United Nations and the Statute of the International Court of Justice*. San Francisco: United Nations Press. https://treaties.un.org/doc/publication/ctc/uncharter.pdf.

United Nations, Security Council, *Letter from the Representative of India Addressed to the President of the Security Council, Dated 1 January 1948*, S/628 (2 January 1948), available from https://digitallibrary.un.org/record/468605/files/S_628-EN.pdf.

United Nations, Security Council, *Letter from the Minister of Foreign Affairs of Pakistan Addressed to the President of the Security Council Dated 15 January 1948 Concerning the Situation in Jammu and Kashmir*, S/646 (15 January 1948), available from https://digitallibrary.un.org/record/469219/files/S_646-EN.pdf

United Nations, Security Council, *Report of Sir Owen Dixon, United Nations Representative for India and Pakistan, to the Security Council*, S/1791 (15 September 1950), available from https://undocs.org/S/1791.

United Nations General Assembly Resolution 181(II)/47, *Future Government of Palestine*, A/RES/181(II) (29 November 1947), available from https://undocs.org/en/A/RES/181(II).

United Nations General Assembly Resolution 390(V)/50, *Eritrea: report of the United Nations Commission for Eritrea; report of the interim Committee of the General Assembly on the report of the United Nations Commission for Eritrea*, A/RES/390(V) (2 December 1950), available from https://undocs.org/en/A/RES/390(V).

United Nations General Assembly Resolution 1514(XV)/60, *Declaration on the granting of independence to colonial countries and peoples*, A/RES/1514 (XV) (14 December 1960), available from https://undocs.org/en/A/RES/1514(XV).

United Nations General Assembly Resolution 2625(XXV)/70, *Declaration on Principles of International Law concerning Friendly Relations and Co-operation among States in accordance with the Charter of the United Nations*, A/RES/2625 [XXV] (24 October 1970), available from https://www.un.org/ruleoflaw/files/3dda1f104.pdf.

United Nations Security Council. 1948. *The India-Pakistan Question*, S/RES/39 (20 January 1948), available from https://undocs.org/S/RES/51(1948).

United Nations Security Council. 1948. *The India-Pakistan Question*, S/RES/47 (20 April 1948), available from https://undocs.org/S/RES/51(1948).

United Nations Security Council. 1948. *The India-Pakistan Question*, S/RES/51 (3 June 1948), available from https://undocs.org/S/RES/51(1948).

United Nations Security Council. 1957. *The India-Pakistan Question*, S/RES/122 (24 January 1957), available from https://undocs.org/S/RES/122(1957).

United Nations Security Council. 1965. *The India-Pakistan Question*, S/RES/211, (20 September 1965), available from https://undocs.org/S/RES/211(1965).

United Nations Security Council. 1971. *The India/Pakistan Subcontinent*, S/RES/307 (21 December 1971), available from https://undocs.org/S/RES/307(1971).

9

Revisiting the United Nations and the Micro-State Problem

ARCHIE W. SIMPSON

The micro-state problem emerged in the late 1960s as many newly independent but very small states applied to join the United Nations (UN). These decolonised micro-states viewed UN membership as a means of confirming their sovereign status, affirming their equality with other states, supplementing their diplomatic connections, and as a means of furthering their security through the UN Charter. Following the principle of self-determination and through the inexorable processes of decolonisation, the post-war dismantling of European empires saw the creation of many new states around the world and by the late 1960s this included many micro-states. Duursma writes, 'due to the decolonisation process the United Nations was confronted with many potential new states of which a great number were rather small territories' (Duursma 1996, 135). The micro-state problem (or 'mini-state problem' or 'micro-state dilemma') was that these very small states (rightly) gained sovereign independence as colonialism ended but they were so weak that they lacked the wherewithal to fully carry out their UN obligations (Schwebel 1973, 109). There were also a number of European micro-states in existence that have not gone through post-war decolonisation, namely: Andorra, Monaco, Liechtenstein, San Marino and the Vatican City.[1] Membership in the UN would mean these micro-states would have the same standing as larger states like Brazil, Canada or India giving them a disproportionate international influence relative to their size. For many diplomats and bureaucrats at the UN this was a problem (Kohn 1967; Gunter 1977, 112–113).

This chapter outlines an episode of UN history that has been largely

---

[1] See: https://holyseemission.org/contents//mission/mission-55e37172a07413.52517830.php.

forgotten. The processes of decolonisation that occurred after 1945 included a wide number of micro-states, and these micro-states sought UN membership to further legitimise their self-determination. This chapter has several sections each detailing aspects of the micro-state problem. The first section offers definitions of micro-states in order to establish the main units of analysis. This is followed by a section that explores the nexus of statehood with self-determination and UN membership. From this, the third section details what the micro-state problem was and provides a detailed account of how the UN responded. A brief section on the post-Cold War period will demonstrate that the micro-state problem was essentially ignored as the size of UN members became irrelevant. The final section will offer some conclusions. The theme of this chapter is that the emergence of many micro-states reflected the norm of self-determination in international politics and that the UN played a significant part in promoting this.

Defining Micro-States

It has been noted by many that there is no consensus as to what constitutes a small state (Benedict, 1967; Amstrup 1976; Archer and Nugent 2002; Ingebritsen et al. 2006; Maass 2009; Archer et al. 2014) including micro-states. This is because there are many ways to define small states, there are many variables that can be used to define small states and because different academics are studying small states for different purposes. Archer and Nugent write, 'ultimately a judgmental element must creep into the exercise of categorising states by size' (2002, 5). Variables like territorial size, population and economic outputs are commonly cited as ways to define small states (Amstrup 1976; Ogashiwa 1991; Crowards, 2002; Ingebritsen et al. 2006; Maass 2009; Archer et al. 2014). Moreover, size is a relative concept in political science as all states are different sizes. Thus, Luxembourg is small compared to Belgium, which is small compared to France, and so on. David Vital (1967) proposed a two-fold means of defining small states involving a combination of industrial/economic capability and population size. Vital argued that small states were either advanced industrial states with populations of 10–15 million or under-developed states with populations of 20–30 million. While this template was formulated during the Cold War, it still has some resonance today.

Within small state studies, the sub-field of micro-states also has a range of competing definitions. Lukaszewski (2011, 74) writes, 'in modern political science there is no consensus as to what might be called the ministates, microstates, small states and finally dwarf states.' A range of scholars have produced different definitions of micro-states including Blair (1967) who uses a population threshold of 300,000 and Plischke (1977) who sets out a twofold format in which micro-states have populations of under 100,000 or between 100,000–300,000 and are UN members. Ali Naseer Mohamed (2002) suggests a threshold of 1.5 million, while Armstrong and Read (1995) use a population threshold of 3 million to define micro-states. However, many scholars indicate that a population threshold of 1 million is sufficient to constitute a micro-state. Scholars such as Gunter (1977), Anckar (2002), Harden (1985), Richards (1990), Warrington (1994), Christopher (2002) and Simpson (2008) use the one million residents or less as a means of identifying micro-states. Though Wivel and Oest (2010, 434) add that micro-states, '[are] permanently stuck as the weak party in asymmetric relationships.' The central point is that micro-states are *very small* states, usually in both population and territorial terms. Moreover, there are important consequences of this smallness such as having smaller governments, fewer economic resources, weaker bureaucracies, smaller militaries, and they are vulnerable to external pressures. Ogashiwa (1991, x) summarises, 'micro-states which have very small populations and land areas also in most cases are economically, militarily and politically vulnerable.'

Statehood, Self-Determination and UN Membership

Initiated by President Woodrow Wilson in 1918, the concept of self-determination was and it became a guiding principle of his 'Fourteen Points' at the Versailles Peace Conference following the First World War. However, it became a principle of international law in 1945 at the insistence of the Soviet Union (Kirgis 1994, 304) and was incorporated into the UN Charter through Articles 1 and 55. Self-determination is, 'the search for full independence and sovereignty by a community with the result to redraw international boundaries at the expense of the existing state' (Danspeckgruber 2002, 3). This means that a 'people' or a 'nation' have the right to possess their own sovereign state. International law, according to Article 1 of the 1933 Montevideo Convention on the Rights and Duties of States,[2] sets out four criteria of statehood: a) a permanent population, b) a defined territory, c) government, and d) capacity to enter into relations with other states (Harden 1985, 51; Simpson 2008; Coggins 2014, 30). Importantly, international law does not specify a minimum threshold for territory or population; this allows for micro-states.

An unwritten fifth criterion is constitutional independence (James 1986) which is essential to self-determination. In 1948 the International Court of Justice set out five criteria for UN membership, namely that applicants a) must be a state, b) be peace-loving, c) accept UN obligations as set in the UN Charter, d) be able to carry out these obligations, e) be willing to do so (Harris 1970,

---

[2] See: https://www.ilsa.org/jessup/jessup15/Montevideo%20Convention.pdf.

28). With UN membership being by application, this placed conditions on membership e.g. the term 'peace-loving' was – in reality – political code for being part of the Grand Alliance that defeated Nazism, thus excluding many states including neutral states.

In 1960, UN membership increased by 17 as decolonisation accelerated and thereafter the rise in membership continued as European empires ended. Self-determination was becoming a norm in international politics and this was being endorsed by the UN. The Declaration on the Granting of Independence to Colonial Countries and Peoples of December 1960 further promoted the ideals of self-determination and encouraged more decolonisation. While in 1961 the Special Committee on the Situation with regard to the Implementation of the Declaration on the Granting of Independence to Colonial Countries and Peoples or 'Committee of 24' was established at the UN to further facilitate decolonisation regardless of state size. This committee offered advice, technical support, and monitored the progress of decolonisation. Throughout the 1960s, many new states gained independence and these states applied to join the UN to further confirm their newly gained sovereign status. By 1967 approximately 20 UN member states out of 123 had populations of less than a quarter million.

In 1965, the UN Secretary-General U Thant in his annual report (United Nations 1965; also Gunter 1977, 110; Duursma 1996, 135) suggested there might be a problem regarding smaller member states. Later, in 1967, he wrote, 'it appears desirable that a distinction be made between the right of [ministate] independence and the question of full membership in the United Nations' (Gunter 1977, 111; Anand 2008, 166). Part of the difficulty was that UN membership activities and obligations were becoming increasingly diverse, more costly and involved more formal commitments such as maintaining permanent missions at the UN. For many newly decolonised micro-states this was problematic as most were economically underdeveloped with small populations, many lacked the diplomatic staff required, and they had domestic issues to deal with following independence. In addition, with the increasing numbers of micro-states joining the UN, there was a concern that UN voting might be distorted; that the micro-states would have a disproportionate influence in international affairs. In 1966 the United Nations Institute for Training and Research (UNITAR) began research into the problems and issues raised by smaller states and territories. The UN Security Council also established a committee of experts, a '*Mini-state committee*', to explore the issue and make recommendations (Gunter, 1977, 111; Harden 1985, 18; Anand 2008, 167). This committee met in secret, issued one interim report in 1970 (Duursma 1996, 136) but came to a stalemate over the micro-state problem, largely because matters of sovereignty and of the legal equality of states were perceived as being particularly sensitive, controversial and difficult. In the context of the Cold War, Soviet dominance in East Central Europe perhaps also illustrated why the committee met in secret.

Explaining the Micro-state Problem

In 1919 and 1920 San Marino, Monaco and Liechtenstein applied to join the League of Nations despite membership being by invitation only (Gunter 1974, 497; Thorhallsson 2012, 144; also, Bartmann 2002, 362). Luxembourg made a successful bid. Monaco failed to supply information to the League and San Marino withdrew its application, but Liechtenstein pursued the matter (Gunter 1974, 497; Harden 1985, 15). The League explored the application asking five important questions (Gunter 1974, 498):

- Is the application in order?
- Is the government recognised *de jure* or *de facto* and by which states?
- Does the country have stable government and settled boundaries?
- Is the country *fully* self-governing?
- What has been the government conduct and assurances over 'international obligations' and 'armaments'?

It was the questions over 'self-governing' and assurances over international obligations (Gunter 1974, 498) that scuppered the application. The Fifth Committee (admissions) concluded that Liechtenstein was a sovereign state but that some, '*attributes of sovereignty*' were carried out by other neighbouring states (Austria and Switzerland) including control of customs, administration of telecommunications, diplomatic representations and decisions in some judicial matters (Gunter 1974, 498; Anand 2008, 164–165). It was also noted that Liechtenstein did not have any armed forces (Bartmann 2002, 362). Such evidence undermined the application and it was concluded that the Principality lacked the capacity to fulfil the obligations of the League. In December 1920 a vote on Liechtenstein's application saw 28 votes against, 1 vote for and 13 abstentions (Gunter 1974, 499). This illustrates that statehood alone was not sufficient in itself for membership; the size of Liechtenstein constrained its capacity to fully adhere to being able to carry out the League's obligations.

A year later, a sub-committee of the Assembly explored the issue of small state membership and suggested three proposals: a) 'associate' membership in which small states had full participation but no voting rights, b) they could be represented by others, and c) 'limited participation' with membership privileges being limited in alignment to cases where their own interests were involved (Harden 1985, 15; Gunter 1974, 499–500). These alternatives were not explored further, and the matter fell into desuetude. Such debates and proposals were replicated by the UN in the late 1960s as the numbers of small states and micro-states increased as a consequence of decolonisation. The micro-state problem for both the League of Nations and the United Nations was that on one hand they were open to sovereign states but on the other hand, the micro-states were less likely or unable to fully fulfil the concomitant obligations that membership required.

After the Second World War, Luxembourg and Iceland joined the UN in 1945 and 1946 as they had sided with the Allies. These micro-states also joined NATO as the politics of the Cold War evolved. In 1949 Liechtenstein applied to become party to the International Court of Justice (ICJ) (Kohn 1967, 556). Members of the UN are automatically party to the ICJ though they can opt-out, but non-members could also be party to the Court subject to recommendations of the Security Council (International Court of Justice 2019). The UN Security Council debated the application and both the Soviet and Ukrainian delegates questioned the sovereignty of Liechtenstein. Their comments echoed the earlier debate of the League of Nations. Kohn (1967, 547) reports that the Ukrainian delegate said:

> Attention must be called to the fact that Liechtenstein does not have an army of its own, as state-like organisations have. At the same time, Liechtenstein has entrusted Switzerland with the function of representing it in its foreign relations. The relationship of Liechtenstein and Switzerland towards each other is not entirely clear to us. We are aware that postal and customs unions exist with Switzerland. But we are not at all clear what considerations led Liechtenstein to entrust Switzerland with its representation abroad – one of the prerogatives of national sovereignty.

The dependence on Switzerland[3] by Liechtenstein with its Western-orientated outlook was problematic for the Soviet Republics and Soviet Union (Kohn 1967, 547–548) given the context of the Cold War. Nevertheless, they did not veto Liechtenstein's admission to the International Court of Justice. Being party to the ICJ allowed the Principality a means to settle disputes with other states and to participate in the wider UN system. But full membership in the UN would occur *after* the end of the Cold War for Liechtenstein and several other European micro-states. However, Monaco gained observer status at the UN in 1956.[4] (Permanent Mission of Monaco, 2019).

---

[3] Switzerland was not a member of the United Nations until 2002 largely to maintain its neutrality.

[4] See: https://mission-un-ny.gouv.mc/Monaco-and-the-UN.

UN membership steadily grew as, 'during the twentieth century, 150 new states entered the international system' (Coggins 2014, 5). This membership accelerated in the 1960s with many smaller states and micro-states gaining independence. This included Trinidad and Tobago in 1962, Malta in 1964, the Maldives in 1965, Barbados in 1966 and Swaziland in 1968. Self-determination was now a norm in international politics as these examples demonstrate. These new states joined the UN and by the late 1960s questions over micro-state membership were raised. The *Mini-state committee* was created to help resolve the micro-state problem.

The *Mini-state committee* received two proposals about dealing with micro-state membership. The first proposal came from the US in 1969 suggesting that a new form of UN membership should be permitted, that of 'associate member' (Anand 2008, 167). This involved five elements (Gunter 1977, 113; Anand 2008, 168):

a) Enjoy the rights of a member in the General Assembly except to vote or hold office.
b) Enjoy appropriate rights in the Security Council upon the taking of requisite action by the Council.
c) Enjoy appropriate rights in the Economic and Social Council and in its appropriate regional commission and other sub-bodies, upon the taking of requisite action by the Council.
d) Enjoy access to UN assistance in the economic and social fields.
e) Beat the obligations of a member except the obligation to pay financial assessments.

This proposal was very similar to earlier suggestions by the League of Nations sub-committee of 1921 on the same issue. However, the proposition was contrary to the one-state one-vote principle that is central to the legal equality of states. In 1970 the British presented an alternative plan in which micro-states would 'renounce certain rights (in particular voting and election in certain United Nations bodies)' (Anand 2008, 168) on a voluntary basis. In addition, 'in return its financial contribution would be assessed at only a nominal level' (Harden 1985, 18). Essentially, the proposal was that the micro-states would voluntarily give up voting rights and consequently pay less for UN membership. The British added that the micro-states could regain these rights if they gave a year's notice and revised their financial contributions. Both the US and Britain argued that their proposals would not require changes to the UN Charter (Anand 2008, 169) although the UN legal counsel thought that the proposals would be difficult to equate with the principle of sovereign equality of states (Thorhallsson 2012, 145). The UN legal counsel also felt that some UN rights were so fundamental that they could not be renounced. A further (political and legal) difficulty was in defining 'micro-states'; the UNITAR study (Rapoport et al. 1971) that began in 1966 included various definitions but the French delegate said, 'that the Committee would have great difficulty in producing any definition at all of a micro-state' (Gunter 1977, 116).

The *Mini-state committee* was established to explore the problem of small states joining the UN because of decolonisation. Two sets of proposals on the issue were produced but neither set of recommendations were commensurate with the UN Charter, and they were unpopular with many small states. In addition, by the time these proposals were made, there were already a number of micro-states in the UN. The micro-state problem could not be resolved, and decolonisation continued into the 1970s. More micro-states joined the UN including Fiji in 1970, Qatar in 1971 and Grenada in 1974. Membership in the UN was viewed as a confirmation of sovereignty and with that, legal equality with other states in international politics. For the micro-states this was particularly important given their diminutive size. This meant that any demotion to *associate status* within the UN was unacceptable to the micro-states. The failure to unravel the micro-state problem became a nuanced historical artefact that had no significant impact upon micro-state membership in the UN.

The Post-Cold War Era

When the Cold War ended in 1989, an opportunity for the European micro-states to join the UN emerged. Seven states joined the UN in the 1980s and six of these were micro-states or small states (Saint Vincent and the Grenadines, Antigua and Barbuda, Belize, Vanuatu, Saint Christopher and Nevis, and Brunei Darussalam) taking membership to 159 states by 1984. This showed that self-determination remained an important principle and was now an established norm. The difficulties of being a micro-state that were central to the micro-state problem were now deemed less relevant. In effect, the outcome of the micro-state committee became more of an academic exercise than anything else. Liechtenstein began lobbying for membership in 1988 and was able to gain membership in August 1990 (Ingebritsen 2006, 120–121). This encouraged other European micro-states to apply for membership. As Duursma (1996, 205) writes:

> Liechtenstein's international behaviour has been in a certain sense a pioneer work for the other European micro-states, because it was the first European micro-state to enter actively into the Council of Europe and the United Nations.

Following Liechtenstein membership, other European micro-states were able to join including San Marino in 1992 and both Andorra and Monaco in 1993. In the 1990s, UN membership saw further increases in membership as the dissolution of the Soviet Union saw the creation of 15 new states including Russia, the velvet divorce of Czechoslovakia occurred and the wars in Yugoslavia further catalysed state creation. While decolonisation was a reason for new states during the Cold War, secessionism became the main reason for new states in the post-Cold War period (Coggins, 2015). Other states were able to join the UN including the Marshall Islands and the Federated States of Micronesia, both micro-states. Other micro-states like Palau in 1994 and Kiribati, Nauru and Tonga joined the UN in 1999. This suggested that the micro-state problem of the 1960s–1970s had been forgotten in the post-Cold War world. However, it also shows that the principle of self-determination remains an ongoing factor in the establishment of new states.

Conclusions

Membership in the UN became universal after the end of the Cold War and the UN now has 193 member states including 44 micro-states and the Vatican City (United Nations, 2018). As a promoter of self-determination and as an instrument for peace and security in global affairs, the UN provides micro-states with an endorsement of their sovereignty. As micro-states have an inherent diminished capacity due to their small size and lack of resources in relation to other states, membership in the UN becomes particularly important. This importance is partly to augment their diplomatic abilities, partly to acknowledge their legal equality with other states, and partly to provide a level of security. The principle of self-determination that became prominent after 1945 was central in establishing many micro-states in the twentieth century. Following decolonisation, membership in the UN was seen as a way in which these micro-states could participate in international politics. It was also seen as legitimising and acknowledging their membership in the international community.

The broader purpose of self-determination when it was established after the First World War was to encourage peace by allowing nations to achieve statehood. In the post-war era, self-determination became an international norm as many new states (large and small) were created as decolonisation occurred. This was encouraged by the UN through various committees, advice given to prospective states, and by the opportunity to join the organisation. As the norm of self-determination encouraged the creation of new states, the UN became the global fulcrum for this encompassing states of all sizes, including micro-states. By promoting self-determination, the UN was successfully empowering colonised territories to achieve sovereign independence. Coggins notes that the international community, '…has swelled to nearly two hundred states' (2015, 15).

The micro-state problem of the late 1960s illustrates that UN membership was not necessarily an automatic process for old or new micro-states. The politics of the Cold War, bureaucratic doubts and the capacity of micro-states to fulfil associated obligations opened up a debate about the micro-states. The existence of European micro-states like Liechtenstein demonstrate that diplomats and bureaucrats at the UN (and previously at the League of Nations) had concerns over whether such micro-states could, in fact, fulfil their international obligations. Such concerns were genuine; however, the ideals of self-determination were, in the long term, a greater catalyst for the growth of micro-states and in UN membership than apprehensions about the capacity of the micro-states. With the constraints of the Cold War over, the (non-decolonised) European micro-states were able to gain UN membership alongside many decolonised micro-states. This contributed to the universal membership of the UN that we recognise today.

References

Amstrup, Niels. 1976. "The Perennial Problem of Small States: A Survey of Research Efforts." *Cooperation and Conflict* 11(3): 163–182.

Anand, R.P. 2008. *Sovereign Equality of States and International Law*. Gurgaon: Hope India Publications.

Anckar, Dag. 2002. "Why Are Small Island States Democracies?" *The Round Table* 365: 375–390.

Archer, Clive, and Neil Nugent. 2002. "Introduction: Small States and the European Union." *Current Politics and Economics of Europe* 11(1): 1–10.

Archer, Clive, Alyson J.K. Bailes, and Anders Wivel, eds. 2014. *Small States and International Security: Europe and Beyond*. London: Routledge.

Armstrong, Harvey, and Robert Read. 1995. "Western European Micro-states and EU Autonomous Regions: The Advantages of Size and Sovereignty." *World Development* 23(7): 1229–1245.

Bartmann, Barry. 2002. "Meeting the Needs of Microstate Security." *The Round Table* 365: 361–374.

Benedict, Burton. 1967. *Problems of Smaller Territories*. London: The Athlone Press.

Blair, Patricia W. 1967. *The Ministate Dilemma*. New York: Carnegie Endowment for International Peace.

Chamberlain, M.E. 1999. *Decolonization*. Oxford: Blackwell Publishing.

Coggins, Bridget. 2015. *Power Politics and State Formation in the Twentieth Century.* New York: Cambridge University Press.

Crowards, Tom. 2002. "Defining the Category of 'Small' States." *Journal of International Development* 14: 143–179.

Danspeckgruber, Wolfgang, ed. 2002. *The Self-Determination of Peoples*. Boulder: Lynne Rienner.

Duursma, Jorri. 1996. *Fragmentation and the International Relations of Micro-States*. Cambridge: Cambridge University Press.

Gunter, Michael M. 1974. "Liechtenstein and the League of Nations: A Precedent for the United Nations Ministate Problem?" *The American Journal of International Law* 68(3): 496–501.

Gunter, Michael M. 1977. "What Happened to the United Nations Ministate Problem?" *The American Journal of International Law* 71: 110–124.

Harden, Sheila, ed. 1985. *Small is Dangerous: Micro-states in a Macro World*. London: Francis Pinter.

International Court of Justice. 2019. "States not members of the United Nations parties to the Statute." Accessed August 1, 2019.
https://www.icj-cij.org/en/states-not-members.

Ingebritsen, Christine, Iver Neumann, Sieglined Gstöhl, and Jessica Beyer, eds. 2006. *Small States in International Relations*. Seattle and Reykjavik: University of Washington Press/University of Iceland Press.

James, Alan. 1986. *Sovereign Statehood*. London: Allen and Unwin.

Kirgis, Frederic L. 1994. "Degrees of Self-Determination in the United Nations era." *The American Journal of International Law* 88: 304–310.

Kohn, Walter S.G. 1967. "The Sovereignty of Liechtenstein." *The American Journal of International Law*, 61(2): 547–557.

Lukaszewski, Marcin. 2011. "Research on European Microstates in Social Science. Selected Methodological and Definitional Problems." *Ad Alta. Journal of Interdisciplinary Research* 1(2): 74–77.

Maass, M. 2009. "The Elusive Definition of the Small State." *International Politics* 46(1): 65–83.

Mohamed, Ali N. 2002. *The Diplomacy of Micro-states*. The Hague: Netherlands Institute of International Relations.

Ogashiwa, Yoko S. 1991. *Microstates and Nuclear Issues: regional cooperation in the Pacific*. Suva: Institute of Pacific Studies of the University of the South Pacific.

Plischke, Elmer. 1977. *Microstates in World Affairs: Policy Problems and Options*. Washington, DC: American Enterprise Institute for Public Policy Research.

Rapoport, Jacques, Ernest Muteba, and Joseph J. Therattil. 1971. *Small States and Territories: Status and Problems*. New York: United Nations Institute for Training and Research.

Richards, Jeff. 1990. "Micro-States: A Specific Form of Polity?" *Politics* 10(1): 40–46.

Schwebel, Stephen M. 1973. "Mini-States and a More Effective United Nations." *The American Journal of International Law* 67(1): 108–116.

Simpson, Archie W. 2008. "Nations and States." In *Issues in International Relations*, edited by Trevor C. Salmon, and Mark F. Imber, 46–60. London and New York: Routledge.

Thorhallsson, Baldur. 2012. "Small States in the UN Security Council: Means of Influence?" *The Hague Journal of Diplomacy* 7(2): 135–160.

United Nations. 1965. *Introduction to the Annual Report of the Secretary-General on the Work of the Organization*. UN doc. A/6001/Add.1. New York: United Nations.

United Nations General Assembly Resolution 1514(XV), *Declaration on the Granting of Independence to Colonial Countries and Peoples*, A/RES/1514(XV) (14 December 1960), available from https://undocs.org/en/A/RES/1514(XV).

Vital, David. 1967. *The Inequality of States*. Oxford: Clarendon Press.

Wivel, Anders, and Kajsa N. Oest. 2010. "Security, Profit, or Shadow of the Past? Explaining the Security Strategies of Microstates." *Cambridge Review of International Affairs* 23(3): 429–453.

Note on Indexing

E-IR's publications do not feature indexes. If you are reading this book in paperback and want to find a particular word or phrase you can do so by downloading a free PDF version of this book from the E-IR website.

View the e-book in any standard PDF reader such as Adobe Acrobat Reader (pc) or Preview (mac) and enter your search terms in the search box. You can then navigate through the search results and find what you are looking for. In practice, this method can prove much more targeted and effective than consulting an index.

If you are using apps (or devices) to read our e-books, you should also find word search functionality in those.

You can find all of our e-books at: http://www.e-ir.info/publications

www.ingramcontent.com/pod-product-compliance
Lightning Source LLC
Chambersburg PA
CBHW020256030426
42336CB00010B/789